D0835045

**THE IOWA
SZATHMÁRY
CULINARY ARTS SERIES**

Edited by David E. Schoonover

P.E.O.
Cook Book

SOUVENIR EDITION

Edited by David E. Schoonover

UNIVERSITY OF IOWA PRESS   IOWA CITY

University of Iowa Press, Iowa City 52242

Foreword copyright © 1992 by

the University of Iowa

All rights reserved

Printed in the United States of America

First paperback edition, 1992

Originally published in 1908 by

Curtis & Gilson, Knoxville, Iowa

Printed on acid-free paper

Library of Congress
Cataloging-in-Publication Data
P.E.O. cook book souvenir
edition/edited by David E.
Schoonover.—
    1st pbk. ed.
        p.   cm.—(The Iowa Szathmáry culi-
nary arts series)
    "Originally published in 1908 by Curtis
& Gilson, Knoxville, Iowa"—T.p. verso.
    Includes index.
    ISBN 0-87745-370-5 (pbk.: acid-free
paper)
    1. Cookery.   I. Schoonover, David
E.   II. Series.
TX714.P17   1992   91-40585
641.5—dc20   CIP

FOREWORD

DAVID E. SCHOONOVER

Kebobbed Oysters and Oyster Short Cake in Iowa? Yes, and Green Corn Balls, Tomatoes Stuffed with Eggs, and P.E.O. Salad! These are some of the more unusual of 575 recipes compiled and tested in 1908 by members of P.E.O. Chapter M in Knoxville, Iowa, and presented in their *P.E.O. Cook Book: Souvenir Edition*. The University of Iowa Press is reprinting this cookbook so today's readers can try these recipes and others, including several pages of hand-written versions for Chilli Sauce, Sponge Cake, and Graham Pudding.

The volume is illustrated with 25 black-and-white photographs of public buildings and private residences in Knoxville. Although eighty-four years have intervened since the book first appeared, it is still possible to identify many buildings from the illustrations. Some architectural details on businesses facing the town square have escaped being "modernized" and the Marion County Court House looks very much the same. Knoxville residents and visitors with an interest in the town's history will enjoy discovering the current condition of buildings and homes pictured.

This book has been selected from a group of several hundred cookbooks in the Szathmáry Collection of Culinary Arts, representing each of the United States. This collection provides a look at American and, in this case, midwestern culinary history at a time when buyers, readers, and collectors of cookbooks may be looking for more than recipes. Many cookbooks also contain introductions, perhaps literary or historical

matter, period advertisements, or a variety of illustrations that
are interesting in themselves. The cultural context of cookbooks is also important—who publishes them, for what audi-
ence, at what time period? For this volume, that context is
clear: members of Chapter M gathered their best recipes to
present to Knoxville and proudly illustrated their book with
pictures of the community.

Early cookbooks also provide information about the
home economics of their time. At least two recipes in this collection seem extraordinarily thrifty: Pressed Chicken for Fifty
requiring three large, fat hens and Creamed Chicken from
four chickens to serve forty people. These cooks express mea-
surements in what now may be unexpected comparisons: they
specify butter the size of an egg for Creamed Shrimps or
butter the size of a hickory nut in Veal Loaf and require alum
the size of a walnut in Cucumber Mangoes. Their directions
are sometimes very general, recommending a quick or brisk
oven or suggesting that Pumpkin Pie be baked rather slowly.
But they can be quite specific: preparation for Graham Bread
demands that the baker sponge one yeast cake at noon.

This particular book has an additional historical Iowa
connection. On January 21, 1869, seven students founded the
P.E.O. Sisterhood in the Music Room of Main Hall at Iowa
Wesleyan University in Mt. Pleasant, Iowa. Mary Allen, Alice
Bird, Hattie Briggs, Alice Coffin, Suela Pearson, Franc Roads,
and Ella Stewart could have joined other associations already
on campus, but Hattie Briggs spoke for the group when she
said, "Let's have a society of our own." From that beginning
the P.E.O. has grown to a membership of more than 240,000,
with chapters across the United States and Canada. Although
the meaning of its initials is secret, the P.E.O. is a philan-
thropic educational organization with international, state, and
local projects.

The University of Iowa Libraries and the University of

Iowa Press are proud to include the *P.E.O. Cook Book: Souvenir Edition* in their Iowa Szathmáry Culinary Arts Series, bringing to readers a taste of midwestern culinary history and emphasizing the P.E.O.'s involvement in an attractive Iowa town.

The P.E.O. Sisterhood

The P.E.O. Sisterhood maintains four educational projects: (1) the P.E.O. Educational Fund, a revolving loan fund established in 1907, lends money to women needing it for education beyond high school; (2) the P.E.O. owns and supports Cottey Junior College for Women, a fully accredited liberal arts college in Nevada, Missouri; (3) the P.E.O. International Peace Scholarship Fund, established in 1949, provides scholarships for foreign students to pursue graduate study in the United States and Canada; and (4) the Program for Continuing Education, established in 1973, provides grants to women in the United States and Canada for purposeful public service or personal educational goals.

Knoxville's Chapter M grew steadily in membership and had a positive impact on the community during the first half of the twentieth century. One member, Dixie Cornell Gebhardt, who had been initiated by Chapter M in 1887, distinguished herself by designing the Iowa state flag, adopted by the General Assembly in 1921. Her contribution permits Knoxville to be known as the birthplace of the Iowa flag. A second Knoxville P.E.O. chapter, LW, was formed in 1966, thus giving additional women the opportunity for membership. Knoxville's P.E.O. chapters continue to focus time, energy, and financial support on educational and civic projects.

ACKNOWLEDGMENTS

I would like to express appreciation to my colleagues at the University of Iowa Libraries for their encouragement and assistance with this project: Sheila Creth, Edward Shreeves, Robert McCown, Susan Hansen, and especially Rijn Templeton and Ann Ford.

For information about P.E.O. activities I would also like to thank Mary Louise Remy, immediate past president of the International Chapter; Deborah Cowan, chief administrative officer at the P.E.O. executive office in Des Moines, Iowa; and Christa Belknap, president of Knoxville's Chapter M, for sharing information about that chapter's projects.

P.E.O. Cook Book

The Old East School Building Built in 1856—Replaced by the Present Building in 1877

A RECIPE FOR A DAY

"Take a little dash of water, cold,
  And a little leaven of prayer,
And a little bit of sunshine gold,
  Dissolved in the morning air.

Add to your meal some merriment
  And a thought of kith and kin,
And then as your prime ingredient,
  A plenty of work thrown in.

But spice it all with the essence of love
  And a little whiff of play,
Let a wise old Book and a glance above
  Complete the well-made day."

TABLE OF WEIGHTS AND MEASURES

One quart flour equals one pound.

Two cups butter equals one pound.

One generous pint of liquid equals one pound.

Two cups granulated sugar equals one pound.

Two heaping cups powdered sugar equal one pound.

One pint finely chopped meats packed hard equals one pound.

Ten eggs equal one pound.

One pound melted butter equals one quart.

One pound and two ounces Indian meal equal one quart.

Four ordinary cups liquid equal one quart.

Four large tablespoons equal one-half gill.

A common sized wine glass holds one-half gill.

An ordinary tumbler holds one-half pint.

NOTICE

To properly care for this book while in use in the kitchen, procure a sheet of window glass, 9x12 inches, and lay over the open book.

SOUPS

TOMATO SOUP [Excellent]

Josie Parsons

To one quart of canned tomatoes add one quart of water and let boil twenty to thirty minutes. Strain through a fruit sieve, add salt and pepper, butter the size of an egg. Now bring to a boil. Remove from fire and add one pint of cream, stirring constantly.—Brought from abroad by Marshall Field's chef.

TOMATO SOUP

Mrs L. S. Woodruff

Stew one quart of tomatoes in one pint of water for twenty minutes; rub two tablespoons of flour and one of butter with a teaspoon of salt, stir into the boiling tomato and cook fifteen minutes. Run through colander and serve with sippets of bread. Cut stale bread into thin slices, butter and cut into small dice. place in pan with buttered side up. Brown crisply in oven.

CREAM TOMATO SOUP

Louem Donley, Chicago, Ill.

Add one quart water to can of tomatoes, cook until very done and run through sieve. Cream one tablespoon of butter into one and one-half tablespoon of flour. Have a quart of cream and milk mixed and when it begins to heat stir in butter and flour. Have in another vessel the tomatoes and when both the tomatoes and milk come to a boil pour together, just before taking off the stove stir in pinch of soda, salt, pepper and a little sugar.

PEA PUREE
Mrs. W. P. Gibson

One can peas rubbed through sieve; one quart milk, one-half cup cream, salt and pepper to taste, bring to a boil. Serve hot with wafers.

GERMAN PEA SOUP
Mrs. C. W. Cornell

Boil good sized shank bone in one gallon of water with one large onion, one stalk celery, one can strained tomatoes, salt to taste. Boil for four hours, then add one pint fresh peas, or one can of peas. Remove onion and ten minutes before serving make drop dumplings: Boil one-half-pint milk, butter size of egg, stir in gradually one-half pint flour while boiling. Remove from fire and add five eggs, stir constantly until smooth, add salt and nutmeg, drop with spoon into broth and boil for a few minutes.

CREAM OF POTATO SOUP
Mrs. W. L. Browne

Cover three good sized potatoes with boiling water; boil five minutes, drain and throw away the water. Cover them with one pint boiling water, add a slice of onion, a bit of celery cut in small pieces. Cook slowly till potatoes are tender. Press all through a colander. Add one pint of milk, pour into double boiler. Mix two tablespoons butter with same of flour. Add to mixture, cook carefully until smooth and season.

CORN SOUP
Prue Collins

Boil one can corn and one and one-half quarts of water for two hours or longer. Strain through fine colander, rubbing pulp of corn through. Place again over fire. Add one cup rich milk, using part of milk with a teaspoon of flour for thickening. Season with butter and salt. The soup when done should be about the consistency of cream. In serving, place a spoonful of whipped cream on each cup of soup.

VEGETABLE SOUP
Mrs. Wm. Shaffner, Burlington, Iowa

Good sized shank soup bone, add two tablespoons of salt, dash of cayenne, one small head of cabbage, one large onion, stalk of celery, stalk of leek chopped fine, can of tomatoes, strained. Drop dumplings; half pint of flour, two eggs, half teaspoon salt, stiff enough to drop with spoon into soup.

CREAM OF CELERY SOUP
Mrs. Maude Mentzer.

One head celery, one pint water, one pint milk, one tablespoon butter, one tablespoon flour, half teaspoon salt, generous pinch white pepper. Clean celery and cut in half inch pieces, put into the pint of water and cook until tender. Mash in water in which it is boiled, adding salt and pepper. Boil milk with small slice of onion. Cream butter and flour and stir slowly into boiled milk. Add this to celery and strain through sieve, pressing through all but the tough fibers of celery. Return to fire and when hot serve.

PUREE BEAN SOUP
Mrs C. M. Harrington.

One-half cup dried beans soaked in three pints of water. Cook until tender and put through colander; add one pint stock, one cup cream, one slice onion, one tablespoon butter, one dessertspoon flour mixed to thicken soup.

BOUILLON
Nette Herrick

To three pounds of raw meat chopped fine add three quarts of cold water. Let it be barely warm for the first hour, then increase the heat and let it gently simmer six hours, stirring occasionally. Turn it into an earthen vessel, salt to taste, cover and let it stand until cool. Skim off all the fat, squeeze the meat hard as you remove it from the liquid. Return the liquid to the fire and boil rapidly for a few minutes. Then strain carefully through a thin cloth. Do not squeeze as it should be a clear amber color.

BEEF SOUP
Mrs. Eli Kaufman

Take a good five-cent soup bone, for six plates of soup. After boiling, skim, then put celery leaves, carrot and tomatoes in and let cook on a slow fire for four hours. Strain it through a colander, put in a half cup of rice, salt to taste, and cook for three-quarters of an hour.

CLEAR SOUP
Elizabeth Councilman

Boil beef soup bone three hours, having two quarts broth; strain. Put over fire to simmer when about ready to serve it. Beat four eggs very little, stir into soup, allowing it to just boil up.

CHILE CON CARNE
Nan Cornell

Two pounds round steak chopped fine, two cups kidney beans, one-quarter pound suet. Soak beans over night. Place over fire with piece of suet. Cook about one and one-half hours, then add meat and chile pepper to taste; add one onion, thicken with flour. Use Gebhardt's Eagle Chile powder.

Marion County Court House

GRAPE SOUP
Mrs. G. W. Baxter, Telford, Tenn.

One pint grape juice, a few raisins (sweeten to suit the taste). Cinnamon bark, about one dozen cloves, a little salt and lemon peeling. Thicken with corn starch (small tablespoon or more if preferred). Add last a slice of bread cut in small squares and fried brown in butter. Remove spice and lemon peeling before serving.

CHERRY SOUP
Emily S. Cooper

One quart of cherries, one cup sugar, one pint of water. Boil and thicken with two tablespoons flour moistened with water.

BEELERUE STEW [Excellent]
Mrs. W. V. Elliott

Two tablespoons butter, one cup celery cut fine, one pint oysters, one cup cream, salt and pepper and cracker crumbs to thicken. The butter is heated in a dish; when hot add the celery, which has been in cold water, cook until thoroughly saturated. Add cream, as soon as heated to the boiling point add seasoning, oysters and cracker crumbs and mix thoroughly. When the edges of the oysters begin to curl it is ready to serve. Garnish with parsley.

NOODLE SOUP   German
Bertha S. Black

Take medium sized shank bone, cover with cold water, add salt and let simmer. Strain one can tomatoes and with one onion, stalk of celery, sprig of parsley, one bay leaf, boil slowly five or six hours. After straining add noodles and let boil up once. Rice or maccaroni soup may be made in the same way.

SOUP BALLS
Mrs. Eli Kaufman

One tablespoon of cold soup fat, put in a bowl and stir to white cream, add three eggs, a pinch of salt and a little nutmeg, one coffee sauce plate of cracker flour. Mix with the above, roll into balls as large as hickory nuts, put in soup half hour before served. Soup must be boiling. Cover air tight.

NOODLES
Mrs. Eli Kaufman

Take one egg, stir with fork, put enough flour in to make it stiff enough to roll up, let it dry and cut as fine as hair. Put in soup five minutes before ready for table.

NOODLES
Mrs. Delia Brobst

One-half cup of sweet milk and one tablespoon of cream, one egg, a pinch of salt and flour enough to make very stiff. Roll very thin and let stand on the board to dry for some minutes. Roll and cut into thin strips. Put into boiling stock and cook until well done.

FISH

"I fished all day and caught—
A cold; and just at night
I had a bite—
(Cold ham and such) 'twas not for naught
I fishing went,
I hooked at least
An appetite."

BAKED LAKE TROUT
Mrs. C. W. Cornell

Place trout in roaster, salt a little. Put thin slices of bacon inside, under and on trout. Sift a little flour over top. Cover and bake slowly one hour. Serve with mustard sauce and garnish with sliced lemon and parsley.

CREAMED SHRIMPS
Maude Wright

One pint milk, butter size of egg, salt and pepper, thicken with flour. When well cooked add one can of shrimps and serve at once on toast.

SALMON LOAF
Blanche Elliott

Mince one can salmon, saving liquor for sauce, put in four tablespoons melted butter, one cup fine bread crumbs, pepper and salt, and finally three or four well beaten eggs. Put in buttered mould and set in pan of hot water, cover and steam for one hour or more. When done set in cold water a minute and turn out. Sauce— Heat one cup milk to boiling, thicken with one tablespoon cornstarch wet in cold water. Add tablespoon butter, salmon liquor and one beaten egg. Take from fire, add juice of one-half lemon, pour over loaf and serve immediately.

SALMON [In Ramekins]
Mrs. E. Hackley, Chicago, Ill.

Butter the ramekins well, then fill with alternate layers of Uneeda crackers (rolled fine) and salmon. Make a dressing of one teacup of milk, a pinch of salt, pepper and teaspoon of butter. Let this come to a boil and pour over the salmon. Bake twenty minutes in a quick oven. Other fish may be prepared in the same way.

SALMON TURBOT AND SAUCE
Josie Boydston

Two cups salmon (large can) made fine with fork, three well beaten eggs, one-half cup sweet cream (or milk and butter), one cup cracker crumbs with one-half teaspoon baking powder, scant teaspoon celery salt, and pepper. Mix thoroughly and put into two well greased baking powder cans: steam one hour. Serve hot.

DRESSING TO SERVE OVER TURBOT

One cup sweet milk, one egg, a scant teaspoon cornstarch, salt, pepper and a speck of cayenne pepper, cook until like gravy, add liquor from salmon. Strain and serve hot.

SALMON SOUFFLE
Mrs. H. L. Bousquet

Chop as fine as possible one large can of salmon with a small onion and a few sprigs of parsley. Blend a tablespoon of butter and the same of flour in a sauce pan. When melted add a gill of sweet cream and the beaten yolks of three eggs. When a little cool add a salt spoon of salt and a pinch of cayenne. Stir in the fish and the whites of the eggs beaten to a firm froth. Pour at once into a buttered baking dish and bake in a brisk oven for twenty-five minutes. It will puff up and be very light and must be served at once from the same dish or it will fall.

SALMON CROQUETTES
Mrs. M. D. Woodruff

One small can salmon, one cup seasoned mashed potatoes, one beaten egg. Form into cakes or balls and dip in eggs, then bread or cracker crumbs. Fry in deep lard to light brown.

OYSTER PIE
Mrs. T. G. Gilson

Line deep pan with pie crust. Put in oysters and liquor, lump of butter, salt and pepper. Put strips of dough to thicken and then an upper crust. Bake until brown. Serve in baking dish.

OYSTER SHORT CAKE
Mrs. H. J. McDonald, Des Moines, Iowa
If this is carefully made it is delicious

Make a rich but light baking powder dough and bake in layer cake tins; split and lightly butter each as it comes from the oven. Scald the strained liquor from a quart of oysters. Rub two tablespoons of butter smooth with two tablespoons of flour and stir into one and one-half cups of scalded milk. Cook and stir until it thickens; add a tablespoon of butter to the oyster juice, heat it, season to taste with salt and white or cayenne pepper. Add oysters and heat until the gills ruffle. Then lay oysters on the layers of shortcake. Add the liquor to the sauce and when blended spread over the oysters; then add another layer of cake, then oysters, and pour sauce over the whole, sprinkle with a little minced parsley and serve very hot.

PIGS IN BLANKETS
Frances Murison, Minneapolis, Minn.

Roll large oysters in cracker crumbs, make a mixture of eggs and milk, season highly with salt and pepper, dip the oysters in this and then again roll in cracker crumbs. Take a ribbon of bacon and put around the oyster, fastening together with a toothpick. Put in oven and bake until bacon is done.

FRIED OYSTERS
Ruby Gamble

Select large fine oysters. Drain and wipe by spreading upon cloth, laying another over them and pressing lightly. Have ready crackers rolled to a powder and seasoned with salt and pepper; also two well beaten eggs. First roll the oysters in crackers, then dip them in the egg and in the cracker the second time. Have a frying pan of lard smoking hot and fry a pretty brown. Place on dish nicely and garnish with parsley.

OYSTER COCKTAIL
Tested

Choose small, fine oysters and allow six to a plate or cup—can serve in either. To each cup cover oysters with a sauce made of one tablespoon lemon juice, one teaspoon of good tomato catsup, one-eighth teaspoon table horseradish, one teaspoon vinegar, one-fourth teaspoon Worcestershire sauce, two drops of tobasco sauce, a little salt. Serve ice cold. Do not mix cocktails until a little while before serving. Serve with wafers.

ESCALLOPED OYSTERS
Kinsley, Chicago

Butter an earthen dish, put a layer of cracker crumbs (not too fine) on the bottom, wet this with some of the oyster liquor; next have a layer of oysters, sprinkle with salt and pepper and lay small bit of butter on them, then layer of cracker crumbs and so on, till the dish is full, the top layer to be cracker crumbs. Beat up an egg adding to it enough rich milk or cream to moisten all. Bake from three fourths to one hour. When baked through uncover and brown.

PANNED OYSTERS
Mrs. Belle Jacob, New York City.

For twenty-five oysters put in a chafing-dish one tablespoon of butter. When it is melted add the juice of half a lemon and one teaspoon of chopped parsley. Then add the oysters, which have been well drained. Stir carefully and cook just enough to make them plump or until the gills are curled a little. Season with salt and pepper. Have toasted bread ready, pour the oysters over it; or cut the toast into small squares, stir them into the oysters and serve directly from the chafing dish.

KEBOBBED OYSTERS
Selected

One pint oysters, one-fourth pint bread crumbs, one teaspoon chopped parsley, one egg, one tablespoon butter, one-fourth cup fine-chopped celery. Beat the egg, dip the oyster in it, then in the bread crumbs. Have ready a buttered baking dish, place a layer of oysters, sprinkle with parsely, celery, salt and pepper; then add another layer of oysters, and continue until all the oysters have been used. Cut butter into small bits, place on top. Bake in quick oven twenty minutes.

OYSTER CANAPES
A. Andresen & Co

Take—one cup cream, four tablespoons bread crumbs, one tablespoon butter, one can cove oysters. Paprika, nutmeg and salt. Boil the cream, add the bread crumbs then butter. Chop oysters fine, add oysters and season it. Serve on Rosettes with olives and little gherkins. Serve hot.

CREAMED OYSTERS IN PATTIES

Lucy Bellamy

Put one pint of oysters into one pint of cold water, one pint of cream or milk in a double boiler over the fire. When cream gets foamy it is hot enough. Put one tablespoon of butter into a sauce pan, stir over the fire until hot, but not brown, then stir in gradually one tablespoon of flour and pour on cream a little at a time, stirring all until smooth. Season with salt and pepper. Add oysters after draining and let remain over fire until gills are curled. When ready to use warm the patties and put one tablespoon in each pattie.

CODFISH BALLS

Mrs. Erma Geist, Joliet, Ill.

Wash salt codfish in water, pick in small pieces to make a cupful. Cut two and one-half cups small pieces of potatoes. Cook potatoes and fish together in boiling water until tender. Drain through sieve, return to stew pan, mash thoroughly and add two teaspoons butter, one egg well beaten, season with pepper and salt if necessary. Beat until very light with fork. Drop by tablespoonsful in smoking hot fat, fry one minute, drain on brown paper and serve.

TARTAR SAUCE

Selected

One tablespoon each of minced sour pickles, onions, capers and parsley, one finely-chopped hard-boiled egg, a very little salt and red pepper, wet the whole with lemon juice and mix with mayonnaise dressing. This sauce is good for fried or boiled fish, boiled tongue, and may be used with fried or boiled meats.

Residence of Dr. N. R. Cornell

MEATS

BEEF ROAST
Mrs. B. A. Gradwohl

Season your roast with salt and pepper, put a little fat into pot, brown on both sides a little, pour over it a cup of water, a piece of onion, a piece of brown bread crust; a little catsup gives a good flavor and nice color. But if you have fresh tomatoes handy drop in, in place of catsup. Let it cook slowly, turn over often and add more water if needed.

VEAL CUTLETS
Mrs. B. A. Gradwohl

Wash your cutlets, season with salt and pepper, dip them into a beaten egg and cracker crumbs, fry in butter a light brown. When brown on one side cover with lid and slowly brown the other side.

GERMAN BEEF ROAST
Bertha Black

Into a sirloin or rump roast insert narrow strips of bacon with a larding needle. Rub with salt and pepper, sprinkle lightly with flour, add cup of boiling water, place one onion in roaster, removing it in one hour, as just a suspicion of onion adds much to the flavor of roast and gravy. Roast in the usual way.

SPARE RIB POT PIE
Alice Bellamy

Cut spare ribs once across and then in strips three or four inches wide, put on in kettle with hot water enough to cover, stew until tender, season with salt and pepper, and turn out of the kettle; replace a layer of spare ribs in the bottom, add a layer of peeled potatoes, (quartered if large), some bits of butter, some small squares of baking powder dough rolled quite thin, season again, then another layer of spare ribs, and so on until the kettle is two-thirds full, leaving the squares of crust for thé last layer; then add the liquor in which the spare ribs were boiled, and hot water if necessary. Cover· and boil half to three-quarters of an hour, being careful to add hot water so as not to let it boil dry.

ROASTED SPARE RIBS
Gertrude McClymond

Salt and pepper, sprinkle sage and flour over ribs, slice three or four onions over all, place in roasting pan with water enough to keep from scorching, baste frequently, cook one and one-half hours. Serve with a tart jelly.

PORK CHOPS AND FRIED APPLES
Florence Gamble

Dust the chops with salt, pepper and a little sage, roll in bread crumbs, fry brown. Pour out part of the fat and put in thick slices of apples that are cut roundwise, brown on one side and turn with a cake turner, finish cooking. Arrange around the platter for a border.

BREADED PORK CHOPS
Ruby Gamble

Dip first in beaten egg, then in cracker or bread crumbs, season to taste and fry in hot lard, turning often until well done   Veal cutlets may be cooked same way.

BAKED HAM
Mrs. Erma Geist, Joliet, Ill.

Select a thick ham weighing fourteen pounds, scrape trim, cover with fresh, cold water, let soak over night. In the morning, drain and dry; prepare a thick dough by mixing flour and water together, roll out to one-half inch thickness and enclose ham in it, wet the edges and press them firmly together; place ham in a large dripping pan and bake slowly in a moderate oven from four to five hours, remove from oven break off shell and skin, trim off any ragged portions, stick fat side with whole cloves in diagonal rows an inch apart, grate the crumbs of white bread thickly over this surface and return ham to oven until a golden brown. Slip a paper frill on the knuckle and serve hot. Ham cooked in this way is cooked in its own juices and is very delicious and no waste.

BREADED VEAL
Ella Kinne

One and one half pounds veal or tender round steak, two eggs, one pint very fine rolled bread or cracker crumbs. The eggs should be beaten lightly and the steak well pounded and seasoned, then cut into pieces the right size to serve one person. Dip the meat first in egg, then the crumbs and fry in hot fat.

GERMAN STUFFED VEAL BREAST
Mrs. C. W. Cornell

Put salt and pepper over and in roast. Make dressing of small, finely chopped onion, browned in butter; moisten crumbs of one loaf of stale bread, half stock of celery chopped, four eggs. After thoroughly heating lift from fire and stuff jacket of breast. Sew up; on top place pieces of butter and little sifted flour. Lay small onion and a few brown crusts of bread in roaster, add a little water; baste frequently. Bake three or four hours, according to size of roast. Garnish with parsley.

FRICANDELLES OF VEAL

Mrs. P. H. Donley, Wichita Kansas.

One-half cup bread crumbs, one-half cup milk; put milk and crumbs over the fire and rub to a paste, then add one pound of chopped veal, one teaspoon salt, one-fourth teaspoon pepper; return to stove and heat through; let cool and form in balls, dip in beaten white of egg and put into frying pan with two tablespoons butter, and fry a nice brown; then put fricandelles in stew pan, and into the butter in frying pan one tablespoon flour, one teaspoon salt, one-fourth teaspoon pepper; to this add one and one-half pints of water or stock, stirring constantly till it thickens; pour over fricandelles in stew pan and simmer one and one-fourth hours.

VEAL LOAF

Mrs. V. E. Risser

Have the butcher chop three pounds of veal and half a pound of salt pork very fine, and add to it three eggs, six small crackers, crushed, two tablespoons of cream, one tablespoon of salt, one tablespoon of pepper, butter the size of a hickory nut. Mix it all well together. Make it into one long roll, put bits of butter over them and bake two hours, basting often with the gravy or water and butter slightly seasoned.

VEAL LOAF

Mrs. Florence Myers.

Three pounds of beef, ground fine, one pint of cracker crumbs, two eggs well beaten, salt and pepper to taste season with sage or onion, enough sweet milk to moisten. Mold into a loaf. Lay thin strips bacon over top. Bake one hour.

TOMATO SAUCE
Dickie Gebhardt.

One tablespoon butter melted; add to this one table-spoon flour. Mix well and add one cup hot strained to-matoes. One teaspoon salt, one-fourth teaspoon pepper. A bay leaf, two cloves and slice of onion added to the tomatoes when cooking are good.

MEAT AND POTATO PIE
(Similar to Chicken Pie)

Mrs. S. F. Cole, Pella, Iowa

Take a nice piece of steak and a small soup bone, cut the steak into small pieces and cook with the soup bone until tender; have plenty of stock for gravy, take out the soup bone, slice into the steak three or four po-tatoes, season well with salt and pepper; when the pota-toes are done, thicken the gravy with flour until it is like cream, turn into a baking dish, make a biscuit dough and cover the baking dish (be sure to make a slash in the dough for the steam to escape.) Bake.

MEAT CROQUETTES
Mrs. Fred. Grant

Meat chopped fine, one-third mashed potatoes, one-half cup of milk, put on stove to boil with one tablespoon of corn starch, celery or onion juice just a few drops, stir all together and let get cold, two eggs beaten up and crackers rolled fine, make the meat in balls, dip in egg, then in crackers and fry in hot lard.

DRIED BEEF GRAVY ON TOAST
Mrs. O. L. Wright

Cut the beef fine and soak in cold water a little while drain and pour over it as much milk as desired for gravy. Let heat slowly. Prepare a thickening of milk and flour, and add it when the milk boils; add a little butter. Pour in a teacup of cream just before removing from fire and pour over pieces of toast. This recipe is good for codfish gravy.

HAM PATTIES
Imogene Bellamy

Chop or grind one cup of boiled or fried ham; mix with an equal quantity of fine bread crumbs and moisten to a soft paste with cream or milk; heat and half fill well greased patty pans. Break an egg on the top of each one, dot with bits of butter, sprinkle with fine cracker crumbs, place in oven and bake until the eggs are set.

This is an excellent way to use up odds and ends of cold meats.

SPICED BEEF (a la mode)
Mrs. H. T. Cunningham

Take a rump roast and use salt pork for larding. By this I mean take a sharp knife and make several deep gashes in the meat, cut pork in little strips and insert in the gashes. Salt and pepper well rubbed in. Put into a stewing kettle small pieces of pork, a piece of onion, carrot, turnip, celery, two bay leaves, six cloves, six allspice, and cayenne pepper; when all is hot place the roast in, sear well on all sides, then add boiling salt water and cook down until done. Serve with caper or cream sauce.

POTTED MEAT
Millie W. Baker, Chicago

One knuckle of veal, one knuckle of beef, two pounds lean meat, cook till meat falls from bone. Pick bones and gristle from meat, then chop or grind very fine. Season with salt and pepper. Have plenty of liquor left, strain, add and heat through. Have quite moist and press in dishes to cool.

VEAL BIRDS
Mrs. Frank Dunlap

Have the veal cut from the leg in thin slices, trim into shape. having the pieces two inches wide and four long; chop the trimmings of veal and pork fine, adding a piece of bacon for each bird, and half as much cracker crumbs as meat, season with salt and pepper and a little onion, add enough egg to hold mixture together, spread on meat, roll and fasten with string or toothpicks, fry until brown in butter, pour one pint of milk in skillet, cover and let simmer thirty minutes.

SWEETBREADS
Mrs. W. C. Mentzer.

Soak sweetbreads over night in salt water. Parboil and dip them into batter made of one egg, flour and milk. Fry in hot butter.

HAMBURG STEAK
Mrs Carl Mulky.

One pound ground round steak, one egg, one tablespoon flour, one-fourth cup milk, salt, pepper, pinch of sugar. Stir all together and fry in balls. Onion to taste.

CHILI CON CARNE
Blanche Elliott

Fry one and one-half pounds round steak, ground fine, in one-half cup lard and butter mixed, keeping the meat broken apart in bits. When cooked thoroughly add one can French Kidney beans, one-half cup water, one generous teaspoonful chili pepper dissolved in little water and salt to taste. Let boil down slowly about ten minutes before serving.

STUFFED MEAT PEPPERS
Mrs. Lois Woodruff

One and one-half pounds lean beef or veal chopped, two tomatoes chopped or one-half cup stewed tomatoes, one cup of bread crumbs, one small onion, two stalks of celery chopped, one tablespoon butter with six cloves in while melting, one tablespoon of Worcestershire sauce. Mix thoroughly; have ready nine green sweet peppers with seeds removed and soaked in salt water for six hours. Stuff peppers with mixture, stand up on points in baking dish; put one-half spoonful of butter or drippings on top of each. Pour a little boiling water around them, bake one and one-half hours.

BEEF BRAINS
Mrs. J. W. Brady

Wash well the brains of one beef. Boil in slightly salted water one half-hour. Let cool, remove the outside membrane, then slice the brains about one-half inch thick. Dip these slices in beaten eggs, then in rolled cracker crumbs and fry in butter.

North Side Public Square

POULTRY AND GAME

"For finer or fatter
Ne'er ranged in a forest,
Or smoked in a platter "—Goldsmith

STEWED CHICKEN
Mrs. Cyrus Mentzer

Cut chicken in pieces as to fry. If very fat remove some of fat after it is partly done. Add plenty of butter and when tender the liquid should scarcely cover the meat. Use good milk, flour and pepper for gravy.

CHICKEN PIE
Margaret Roberts

Select a good sized fowl, joint it, cover well with boiling water, so as to have plenty of liquor for the gravy, season with salt and pepper, cook until tender, lift out of the liquor into a good sized dripping pan, sprinkle a little more salt and pepper, and a few bits of butter over it. Put enough flour to thicken the liquor—about two tablespoons into a bowl, and a cup of rich milk, the beaten yolk of an egg, a lump of butter; stir into the boiling liquor, pour over the chicken enough to cover it. Reserve enough gravy for the pie absorbs some. To make dumplings, sift one pint of flour with teaspoon of baking powder, add pinch of salt, piece of lard size of walnut, rub together, mix with buttermilk to which has been added a pinch of soda, knead lightly, roll to one-half inch thickness, cut into small diamond shapes, lay over the chicken. Bake in a hot oven until nicely brown; then serve.

NEVER-FAILING CHICKEN POT PIE
Mrs. Lena Cornell

Sift one pint of flour, one heaping teaspoon baking powder, one-half teaspoon salt; add enough sweet milk to make soft dough. Roll an inch thick, cut hole in center with biscuit cutter. Remove chicken from broth, add a little milk thickened with flour to broth and place pot pie in pot. Cover and let boil a half hour.

CHICKEN PIE
Mrs. Alice Stentz

Stew chicken until it falls from bone, chop fine, put in baking dish; thicken broth—stir through chicken.

CRUST

Two eggs, two cups sweet milk, two tablespoons butter, two cups flour, two teaspoons baking powder; beat eggs and butter thoroughly, add milk, flour and baking powder. pinch of salt; have chicken hot, pour batter over it—bake in quick oven.

CHICKEN PIE
Mrs. Elizabeth Davies

Stew chicken until tender. Line the sides of a deep pan with a nice pastry, put in the chicken and the liquor in which it was boiled, which should be but one half pint, season with a large piece of butter, salt and black pepper. Then cover loosely with crust. While this is baking have ready one quart of fine oysters; put on the fire one pint of rich milk, let it come to a boil, thicken with a little flour, season with butter, salt and pepper, pour this over the oysters boiling hot. About fifteen minutes before the pie is done lift the crust and pour the oysters and all into the pie. Then return to oven and finish.

CHICKEN CROQUETTES
Willa Underhill.

Two tablespoons butter in sauce-pan, blend with this three tablespoons flour. In a cup beat two eggs, fill half full of milk, add to the butter and flour. In this add a cup of chopped cold chicken, a little chopped onion and cook five minutes. When cold mold into croquettes and roll in cracker crumbs and fry in hot fat.

CREAMED CHICKEN
Mrs. R. G. Emmel, Harvey, Iowa.

One four-pound chicken cooked in water until very tender, four sweetbreads cooked until tender. When cold remove chicken from bones and cut in small pieces. Chop the sweetbreads. Make a white sauce of four cups milk, three tablespoons butter and three heaping table spoons flour, salt and pepper. In the bottom of a two-quart pan put half of the cream sauce. Add next the chicken and sweetbreads. Cover with the remainder of the sauce. On the top spread cracker crumbs previously moistened with melted butter. Bake about twenty minutes. Nice for luncheons.

CREAMED CHICKEN
Dell McDonald, Des Moines, Iowa

Four chickens (hens preferred). One quart cream, three tablespoons flour stirred in water. Heat cream hot. Season with salt and pepper. Stir chicken, skin included. After being chopped very fine place in dish and pour above cream over it. If not moist enough add one teaspoon chicken oil and a little flour and water. Place all in oven to brown over a little. Serve hot. This will serve forty people.

CREAMED CHICKEN
Miss Prudence Collins

One chicken weighing four and one-half to six

pounds, one can of mushrooms. Boil chicken, and when cold cut up as for salad. In a saucepan put four coffee-cups or one quart of cream. In another four large tablespoons of butter and five even tablespoons of flour. Stir until melted; then stir into cream until it thickens. Flavor with nutmeg and salt. Put chicken, cream and mushrooms into baking dish, cover with grated bread crumbs and pieces of butter. Bake twenty minutes.

SMOTHERED CHICKEN
Mrs. E. R. Beitzell Des Moines, Iowa

Cut up chicken as for frying; lay in buttered roasting pan with plenty of butter in lumps and salt and pepper. Cover and roast until tender.

OYSTER DRESSING WITH FRIED CHICKEN
Mrs. C. C. Cunningham

Fry the chicken brown on one side and as soon as it is turned cover with the following dressing and bake in the oven thirty minutes: Three cups cracker crumbs, one cup bread crumbs, one cup cream, pepper and salt to taste, butter size of a walnut, juice of pint of oysters (fresh or cove), mix thoroughly, add the oysters and cover the chicken.

FRENCH FRIED CHICKEN
Mrs. Frank Dunlap.

Take one tablespoon of lard and one of butter, let it get hot. Take chicken that has been cut up, salted and rolled in flour, brown chicken very little in this, then add quart of milk and let simmer slowly until done. It will make its own gravy.

PRESSED CHICKEN
Mrs. Elizabeth Stevens

Cut chickens in pieces and boil until the meat will readily drop away from the bones. Remove meat from bones. Chop fine the dark and light meat separately, adding salt and pepper to taste. Boil down liquor in which chicken was cooked until there is about enough to thoroughly moisten chopped chicken. Pour over chicken hot, mixing well. Pack closely in a dish or crock alternating with a layer dark then of white meat, a plate pressed firmly down on it until cold. Slice and serve.

PRESSED CHICKEN FOR FIFTY
Mrs. P. M. Stentz

Three large, fat hens, thoroughly cleaned and cooled, salt and cook until very tender. Cook down well in broth. Separate the light and dark meat, and grind through meat grinder. If broth is rich skim off a part of the fat, and add a lump of butter to flavor, then add one quart of cold water, let heat and use to mix meat. Take white meat, season well, add liquor, let it take up all it will. Take dark meat season with salt, pepper and celery salt, then add liquor, mix very soft, measure your meat, put one bowl of white meat in pan and press, then one bowl of dark, and so on until all is used. Press gently with the hand and let it cool. Do nor put on a weight.

CHICKEN AND GREEN CORN PIE
Burnie Woodruff

Slice the corn from twelve tender but well filled ears and scrape the cobs well. Have ready one chicken nicely fried, one pint of fresh milk, one gill of sweet cream, two ounces of butter, three fresh eggs. Put one-third of the corn in the bottom of a baking dish, sprinkle with salt and pepper, using one third of the butter cut into bits. Lay over this one-half of the chicken. Add another layer of corn, salt, pepper, butter, and chicken. On this put the rest of the corn, seasoning and butter.

Beat the milk, eggs and cream together and pour over the pie just as you are ready to put it into the oven. Bake thirty minutes and serve at once.

CHICKEN MOUSSE
Dixie Cornell Gebhardt

Strain one cupful of hot, highly-seasoned chicken stock over the beaten yolks of two eggs and cook in double boiler until it thickens like cream. Add to this one cup of seasoned, finely chopped chicken, a large tablespoon of minced mushroom, stirring constantly. Remove at once from the fire. Have one tablespoon of gelatine (granulated preferred) which has been dissolved in a little cold chicken stock, ready to mix with this. Whip one cupful of cream; then carefully mix with the beaten cream the stiffly beaten whites of three eggs. Stir this with the gelatine into the chicken mixture and beat until nearly set. Pack in a wet mold and set on ice to chill. When serving cut in slices and arrange on lettuce leaves. Put a spoonful mayonnaise dressing on each slice. Pretty to surround each piece with celery salad.

CHICKEN AND NOODLES
Mrs. J. S. Bellamy

Joint and boil a good fat chicken in plenty of water until tender. Season while cooking with salt and a little cayenne pepper.

For the noodles sift one cup of flour, one-half teaspoon of baking powder, and one-half teaspoon of salt into a pan. Rub one egg through this, add a very little sweet milk, just enough to make into a stiff dough. Roll out as thin as possible; this will make two large sheets. Flour well and fold and roll the sheets and cut in fine strips. Mix one table spoon of flour in a little milk, add to the chicken and boil up. Remove most of the chicken,

add some of the noodles, then part of chicken, alternating until all is used. Stew gently for about twenty minutes, when it is ready to serve.

ESCALLOPED CHICKEN
Mrs. Mell Woodruff

Take one and one-half pints of cold chicken ground
in meat chopper, one-third as much dry bread ground,
one hard boiled egg chopped fine, and one beaten egg,
salt and pepper to taste. Butter size of egg. Add eggs
according to amount of chicken used and milk sufficient
to cook. Bake in oven.

HOT TAMALES
Mrs. W. P. Gibson

Cook a quart of corn meal mush thoroughly, add one-
half cup butter last thing. Chop fine three pounds chicken
or veal, two onions, three or four large red peppers, salt
to taste, cup of chopped raisins, and one of nuts. Cut
corn husks square at ends and long as possible. Dry
husks obtained at any elevator, must be boiled to fold
well. Spread on a cake of mush, fill with chopped meat,
fold into a little roll. Fold both ends over and tie with a
bit of husk. Serve hot from steamer.

ROAST TURKEY
Elizabeth Hiller, Cooking School Instructor

Select a plump, young, ten-pound turkey, dress,
clean, stuff and truss. Place it on a rack in a dripping
pan, rub entire surface with salt and spread with a butter
paste, made by creaming together one-third cup butter
and adding slowly one-fourth cup flour. This is spread
over breast, wings and legs. Place in a hot oven and
brown delicately, turning turkey often. Reduce heat
when evenly browned, add two cups water to fat in the
pan and baste every fifteen minutes until turkey is cooked.

This will require from three to three and one-half hours,
depending somewhat upon the age of the bird. For first
basting, after turkey is delicately browning, use one-half
cup melted butter in one cup boiling water. If turkey is
browning too rapidly, cover with a piece of heavy paper
well buttered, placing over turkey, buttered side down.
Remove the skewers and strings used in trussing before
serving.

ROAST GOOSE
Mrs. C. W. Cornell

Rub pepper, salt and celery salt over and inside
goose. Prepare a dressing of one loaf of stale bread,
soaked then squeezed dry, a small onion, stalk of celery
cut fine, browned in butter. To this add the bread, four
eggs, stir until heated, remove from fire, stuff goose and
sew up. Put a small onion in roaster, cover and bake
slowly one hour. Remove grease, sift a little flour on
top. Add a little water and a few crusts, then bake three
hours. Cover giblets with water and cook tender and cut
in small pieces. Make a little thickening of flour and
water, and with giblets add to gravy.   Serve with apple
sauce. Garnish with parsley.

BRACE OF DUCKS
Elizabeth Hiller, Cooking School Instructor

Dress and clean a brace of wild ducks, stuff and
truss. Fill with apple and bread stuffing, place on rack
in dripping pan, sprinkle with salt and pepper, cover
breast and legs with very thin slices of fat salt pork.
Cook rare twenty-five to thirty minutes in a very hot oven
basting every five minutes with the drippings in pan.
Serve with olive or orange sauce. Currant, wild plum or
green grape jelly should accompany a duck course. Wild
birds are seldom stuffed. Domestic ducks are properly

Residence of G. K. Hart

filled with this stuffing and should be well cooked, requiring more than twice the time required for the cooking of wild ducks.

QUAIL
Burnie Woodruff

Clean and split down the back, wipe carefully. Season well with salt and pepper and place on gridiron over a clear, hot fire, turn and when done lay on a hot dish, butter well and serve on buttered toast.

RABBIT IN BATTER
By Request

Disjoint rabbit and bone it. Dip in batter and fry. Make the batter as follows: One-half pound of flour, season to taste, add two tablespoons of melted butter, a breakfast cup of tepid water and the yolks of two eggs. Mix all together. Let it stand for some hours. Beat the whites stiff and add the last thing.

SQUABS ON TOAST
Mrs. Kate Crawford

Prepare squabs as you would chicken to roast. If squabs are old par-boil about fifteen or twenty minutes. Make a good bread dressing, using oysters if you like, fill squabs, place in double roaster and bake about thirty or forty minutes. Serve on crisp pieces of toast with a little of the gravy poured over them. Garnish with parsley.

GERMAN NOODLES
Mrs. C. W. Cornell

One pint flour, five eggs, one-half teaspoon salt; mix thoroughly, divide into three portions, rolling each into a thin sheet. Let dry. Roll layers up and cut in very thin strips. Drop into boiling salt water, let boil ten minutes, then drain in colander. Place on platter and put on top cracker crumbs browned in butter. Garnish with parsley.

BREAD STUFFING OR DRESSING
Dickie Cornell Gebhardt

Cut the brown crust from slices or pieces of stale bread, put it into a suitable dish or crock and pour cold or tepid water or milk (not warm, for that makes it heavy) over it; let it stand a minute as it soaks very quickly. Now take up a handful at a time and squeeze it hard and dry with both hands, placing it, as you go along, in another dish. When all is pressed dry, toss it all up lightly through your fingers. To one loaf of bread add pepper, salt—about a teaspoonful—also same amount of sage if liked. Add small half-cup of melted butter, two well-beaten eggs, also large cup of oysters if for turkey or chicken. For geese or ducks omit oysters, adding a few slices of onion. Always soak bread in cold liquid as hot makes it heavy.

APPLE AND BREAD STUFFING

To three cups stale bread crumbs, broken in pieces, add three cups apples pared and cut in one-fourth inch cubes, two and one-half tablespoons chopped onion, one-fourth teaspoon powdered sage, two tablespoons butter, one-fourth teaspoon pepper, one teaspoon salt. Mix apple, bread crumbs and onion, sift in dry ingredients, add butter melted, mix lightly with a fork and fill wild or domestic ducks or goose. Large seeded raisins may be added.

DROP DUMPLINGS
Lizzie H. Underhill

One-half tea-cup cream, one-half tea-cup of milk, one egg, two heaping teaspoons baking powder sifted with a little flour. Add flour until batter is thick enough to drop without dripping from a spoon. As soon as done lift out with perforated spoon and break open immediately with a sharp tined fork.

DUMPLINGS

Mrs. O. L. Wright.

To serve with stewed chicken or meat. Beat one egg very light, one teacup of sour milk (half or all of it sour cream preferred) one teaspoon soda, added to one teacup of flour and a little salt sifted together and thoroughly beaten into the milk and egg, add enough more flour to make a batter that will drop from spoon in a lump. When the broth is seasoned let it boil briskly and dip your spoon first into it then into batter to keep it from sticking. When done lift them out with wire egg beater into a hot platter and immediately break open with fork and they will not be soggy. Thicken broth for gravy and pour same over dumplings. Sweet cream and baking powder may be substituted.

DROP DUMPLINGS

One pint milk, two eggs, three teaspoons baking powder, flour to make batter.

VEGETABLES

"He eateth corn from off the cob,
With smile from ear to ear"

FRICASSEED CORN
Mrs. Geo. P Anthes

Cut fresh corn from the cob; put in a pot and just cover with boiling water. Let it boil half an hour, mix in a half pint of cream, a tablespoon of butter, one of flour a little salt and pepper, and let it boil a few minutes

GREEN CORN BALLS
Mrs. C. Mulky

Grate enough green corn from the cobs to make two cupsful, stir a beaten egg, a teaspoon each of sugar and melted butter, add enough flour to form the mixture into balls. Roll in cracker crumbs and fry in deep fat.

GREEN CORN FRITTERS
M. M. G.

One pint of tender green corn rasped from the ear with a coarse grater, one cupful milk, two well beaten eggs, one-half cup sifted flour, season well with salt and pepper, add one teaspoonful of butter. Beat all well together and fry in hot butter, making each fritter of one large spoonful of the batter, brown on both sides.

CORN FRITTERS
Tested

One pint corn or one can, one egg, one-half cup milk, one-half teaspoon salt, one teaspoon baking powder one scant cup flour. Fry in hot fat.

CORN FRITTERS
Mrs, J. S. Bellamy

Stir into one can of corn, two eggs, a tablespoon of butter, a little sugar, salt and pepper, one cup of milk, and enough flour to make a thin batter. Bake until brown.

ESCALLOPED CORN
Mrs. Maude Mentzer

Put a layer of broken up crackers in a buttered bake dish, then a layer of corn, fresh or canned, lumps of butter, salt and pepper, another layer of crackers, then corn and crackers, then enough milk to moisten all. Bake twenty minutes with grated bread crumbs on top.

POTATOES AU GRATIN
Mrs. L. S. Woodruff

One pint of cold boiled, seasoned potatoes. Cut into a quarter of an inch dice. One cup of white sauce, half cup of crumbled cheese, the same of cracker crumbs, one tablespoon of melted butter. Place the potatoes into a shallow dish, suitable for serving, then add the cheese and white sauce. Cover with the cracker crumbs, moisten with the melted butter, bake until the crumbs brown.

WHITE SAUCE

Mix two tablespoons of sifted flour with two of warm butter. Place over the fire a sauce pan containing a pint of sweet milk and a half teaspoon of salt, and a dash of white pepper. When it reaches the boiling point, add the butter and flour, stirring briskly until it thickens. Cook about five minutes.

POTATO STRAWS
Mrs. Maude Mentzer

Pare and slice old potatoes and let stand in cold water for one hour. Cut in thin strips and fry a delicate brown in deep fat; season with salt. Makes a pretty border for platter of chops or steak.

BAKED POTATOES
Mrs. H. M. Antrobus

Select several smooth potatoes, wash thoroughly and bake in moderate oven. When done, cut off top and dig out potato (be careful not to break hull). Season with salt, butter and cream or rich milk. Add the well beaten white of one egg and one teaspoon baking powder. Beat thoroughly. Fill hulls, put tops in place, stand on end in pan, put in oven and heat thoroughly. Very nice.

POTATO DUMPLINGS
Mrs. G. W. Baxter, Telford, Tenn

Grate three of your largest cooked potatoes, then grate eight large raw potatoes, drain through a tea towel, use the starch that has settled on the bottom of the pan for mixing raw and cooked potatoes, one-fourth teaspoon of salt. Roll in balls, put in a kettle of boiling water. Cook one-half hour. Put browned bread in balls.

POTATO PUFFS
Ella McClure

Two cups mashed potatoes, two tablespoons butter, two eggs, one cup cream, salt and pepper. Beat the eggs until light, melt the butter and stir into eggs. Beat this mixture into potatoes, then add cream and seasoning and beat all until light. Grease gem pans and have each half full of mixture. Bake in a quick oven until brown. Serve immediately.

CREAMED POTATOES
Aimee Cornell

Cook one-half dozen potatoes with jackets on and when cold cut into cubes. Make a dressing of one teaspoon flour in one-half pint milk and butter size of an egg, salt and pepper and chopped parsley. Put potatoes in dressing and heat.

POTATO FRITTERS

Mrs. C. W. Cornell

Pare and grate six large raw potatoes. Add two eggs, well beaten, one-half teaspoon of salt, one tablespoon flour four tablespoons of sweet milk. Have plenty of lard smoking hot in skillet, and fry a golden brown. Serve with porter house steak and mushrooms.

GERMAN POTATO BALLS

Mrs. C. W. Cornell

Boil one dozen potatoes night before using. Next morning skin and grate, add five eggs, salt to taste. Sift in enough flour to make firm. Form balls size of an orange, putting three small cubes browned bread inside. Drop in boiling salt water and let boil forty minutes. Serve with game or meat with plenty of delicious gravy.

HASHED BROWN POTATOES

Mrs. W. V. Elliott

Mince cold boiled potatoes not too fine. Cook in a sauce made of butter, flour and milk, using a tablespoon each of flour and butter to one cup of milk. Season well and simmer the potatoes until the sauce is nearly absorbed. Draw to one side, butter the pan and turn potatoes into buttered surface. Cook until a buttered crust is formed and serve on a hot platter like a folded napkin.

POTATO BALLS

Nora Elliott

One pint mashed potatoes, one tablespoon butter, one tablespoon grated cheese, one level teaspoon salt, a pinch of cayenne, one level teaspoon of onion juice, one well beaten egg. Roll in dried crumbs and fry.

SWEET POTATOES WITH DRESSING
Mrs. C. Mulky

Pare sweet potatoes and put in one-fourth cup of sugar, one pint of milk and water together, one heaping tablespoon of lard. Put in all together and boil until done.

COLD SLAW

Soak small head of cabbage in cold water one hour. Shave very fine, salt, pepper and sugar to taste; stir with a fork, pour over this a small cupfull of thick sour cream and enough vinegar to suit the taste.

HOW TO PREPARE SWEET POTATOES
Mrs. George Anthes

Take large potatoes and put them on to boil or steam. When nearly done take out and peel. Slice not quite half an inch thick. Put in a baking pan with a very little water, sprinkle white sugar thickly over them and spread each slice with butter. Set them in the stove to brown.

BAKED CREAMED CABBAGE
Mrs. Nora Elliott

One small head cabbage well cooked; season with salt and pepper. Mix with white sauce. Cover top of pan with rolled bread crumbs, cover with small bits of butter and grated cheese. Bake one-half hour.

ESCALLOPED CABBAGE
Mrs. John Pullman, Silver City, Iowa

Chop cabbage fine, salt and pepper; a layer of cabbage and a layer of either bread or cracker crumbs. Repeat until the dish is full. Pour milk or cream and butter over the top. Bake one and one-half hours.

West Ward School Building

FRIED TOMATOES
Josie Parsons

Pare and core nice smooth tomatoes, fill the centers with butter, sprinkle with salt and place in frying pan over a slow fire. When thoroughly cooked put two tablespoons of thick cream on each one and serve hot.

BAKED TOMATOES
Mrs. Eugenia Hackley, Chicago, Ill.

Butter the ramekins and place in each a large tomato with the center scooped out. Mix with that which has been removed, a cup of bread crumbs, salt to taste, tablespoon of butter and small spoon of flour. Refill the tomatoes and bake in quick oven fifteen minutes.

BAKED TOMATOES
Mrs. J. B. Elliott

Select good-sized tomatoes. Scoop out the inside. Take six ears of sweet corn, cut off upper portion of kernels and scrape ears. To them add a cup of butter beans, moisten with cream and season with salt, stir in half pint bread crumbs. Fill the tomato cups. Bake.

TOMATOES STUFFD WITH EGGS
Mrs. Anna Cunningham

Select as many round, smooth, firm tomatoes as there are persons to be served. Wash, cut a thin slice from the top of each and lay aside for cover. Hollow out a sufficient space to admit an egg. Put in each a little piece of butter, drop in an egg, taking care not to break the white or yolk, season with salt and pepper, place a dot of butter on top of egg, replace the top and bake about twenty minutes or until tomato is tender. A little cheese may be sprinkled over the tomatoes.

MINCED TOMATOES
Mrs. J. B. Elliott

Take as many green peppers as there are people to serve. Cut off tops and scoop out inside. Boil fifteen minutes. Chop fresh tomatoes and mix with minced ham, two parts tomatoes to one part ham. Add to this one teaspoon finely chopped onion, dash of cayenne, a spoon of salt and a little sugar. Put in peppers and bake twenty minutes. Place piece of butter on each. Serve hot on toast.

BOSTON BAKED BEANS
Mrs. J. A. J. Powers

One quart of beans carefully picked over and soaked over night in cold water. In the morning put them over the fire in fresh, cool water and parboil slightly, drain off water and dash cold water over them. This gives them a firmness which prevents them breaking and also gives them a good flavor. Lay a thin slice of fat pork in bottom of bean pot, on this a small onion, pour in the beans, lay a piece of salt pork in the center buried in beans, then add a little salt, if needed. One teaspoon of ground mustard, two tablespoons of sorghum molasses, cover with cold water and bake slowly one-half day. If the oven is too hot cover over top of pot; if water cooks away rapidly, replace with hot water, but do not add water for at least thirty minutes before taking out of the oven. They should be a reddish brown, tender and whole when done. Excellent.

BAKED BEANS
Mrs. J. F. Mentzer

Wash and soak over night one pint of beans. In the morning barboil slightly, put in fresh water, season with salt, pepper and a little sugar, lay on top several strips of sliced bacon, or fresh pork ribs. Cover closely and cook until meat and beans are tender. Put in baking pan in quick oven, meat on top and bake a nice brown.

BOSTON BAKED BEANS
Mrs. J. Risser

Soak beans in tepid water over night. Parboil early in morning with bit of soda in fresh water. Let boil up a few minutes. Put in colander and pour cold water through. Put small onion in bottom of open bean pot, then thick layer of beans with salt, pepper and little sorghum, a two-pound piece of pork chops, then more layers of beans with seasoning. Over all one-half cup tomato catsup. Bake at least six hours.

GERMAN SPINACH
Mrs. C. W. Cornell

Boil spinach in salt water until tender. Pour in colander, let drain, press dry with spoon. Place on meat board and chop with knife. Put tablespoon of butter in skillet, small onion finely minced, spoonful of flour, let brown, add beef broth or water to make gravy. Add spinach. Season with salt and pepper. Let boil a few minutes. Turn into a tureen and garnish with sliced hard boiled eggs.

FRIED PARSNIPS
Eva Belville

Boil parsnips in salted water until tender, cut in long slices, dip in egg, roll in corn meal and fry like fish.

TO COOK PARSNIPS
Mrs. Geo. P. Anthes

First scrape parsnips, slice lengthwise and parboil, then place them in a long baking pan, with just enough water to prevent them from burning. Sprinkle brown sugar over them and place strips of fat bacon on the parsnips to season, bake until brown. On taking them up, pepper well and lay aside the bacon.

FRIED ONIONS
P. E. O. Cook Book, Oskaloosa

Let the whole onions stand in cold water, slice into a stew pan and put on back of the stove, covered closely, to steam one hour. Do not put any water on them, as the steam will make plenty of moisture. After steaming one hour, add a good-sized piece of butter, salt and pepper. Serve at once.

CREAMED ONIONS
Blanche Elliott

Cut off tops of young onions, wash, remove outer layer of skin and boil one-half hour in fresh hot water, drain, press through colander, add two pints sweet milk to one cup onion pulp, thicken with one heaping table-spoonful flour, blended with one of butter. Season with salt, pepper, one teaspoonful parsley. Cook three minutes.

BAKED ONIONS
By Request

Select firm onions of medium size, place in baking dish with a little water. Do not remove skins. Cover closely and bake in a moderate oven for one and one-half hours or until tender. Take from oven, remove skins, season with butter, salt and pepper. Serve hot.

ASPARAGUS ON TOAST
Mrs. A. B. Culver.

Tie stocks in small bunches, boil in salt water until tender. Toast as many slices of bread as there are bunches of asparagus, butter while hot, lay bunch on each slice of toast and pour drawn butter over all.

DRAWN BUTTER

One tablespoon butter, one of flour, mix to a smooth paste, add cup of boiling water, cook until it thickens, add salt and pepper.

South Side Public Square

ASPARAGUS ON ROSETTES
Alfred Andresen & Co

Place asparagus on the Rosette, cover with thick cream sauce; press the whites of hard boiled eggs through a potato ricer over it, then the yolks, pressed through a ricer and dust on top finely cut parsley. Serve as a separate course. Any vegetable with a cream sauce can be served in the same way.

RICE AU GRATIN
Mrs. W. H. Lyon

To one cup of rice steamed, allow one tablespoon salt, cover bottom of baking dish with a layer of rice; dot over with three-fourths tablespoon of butter, sprinkle with a thin layer of grated mild cheese and a slight sprinkle of cayenne. Continue alternate layers until rice and one-fourth pound of cheese are used; pour on milk hot to half the depth of the baking dish. Cover with buttered cracker crumbs and bake in oven until cheese melts and crumbs are browned. Use one-third to one-half cup butter to cup of bread.

FRIED EGG-PLANT
Mrs. Mary Anthes

Peel a nice, large egg-plant, cut in thin slices, lay in salt water two or three hours, then steam until tender. Make a batter of two eggs, first beaten separately, then together; a teacupful sour cream, a teaspoonful of salt, half a teaspoonful of soda and flour to thicken. Dip the slices of egg-plant in the batter and fry in boiling lard until a light brown.

GREEN PEAS
Mrs. Bertha Black

Shell one gallon peas, cover with water, boil one hour, leaving just enough water to keep from burning. Add one-half teaspoonful of salt, one of sugar, butter size of an egg. Let simmer ten minutes and serve,

SALSIFY OR OYSTER PLANT
Mrs. G. P. Anthes.

Wash, scrape and slice in round pieces, boil in salt water until perfectly tender, then drain off the water, pour over a little cream together with a piece of butter rolled in flour, season with pepper and a little salt, let simmer a few minutes, take off and pour over a little vinegar sweetened with sugar. Mix well and serve hot, in a covered dish.

CREAMED SPINACH
Selected.

Wash and cook twenty minutes, drain, chop very fine and drain again, Season with salt and pepper and return to the fire; stir in two tablespoons cream and two tablespoons butter and cook a minute longer and serve very hot.

A NICE WAY TO SERVE CAULIFLOWER
Mrs. S. C. Johnston

Select a nice, large head of cauliflower. Soak in salt water for one hour (do not cut up) then place in your kettle and cook until tender; lift from water and drain, then place in a round baking dish and make a cream dressing (of one pint of milk or cream, a piece of butter, boil and thicken with a spoonful of flour stirred smooth in cold water), pour this over the cauliflower. Take stale bread, crumble fine and mix with melted butter. Cover well with this and set in the oven until hot and a nice brown.

CREAMED MUSHROOMS
Adda Roberts

Clean twelve large mushrooms and put them in a buttered shallow pan, setting them cup side up. Sprinkle them with salt and pepper and dot them over with butter. Add two-thirds cupful of cream and bake ten minutes. Nice with toast.

SALADS

P. E. O. SALAD. (Yellow and White)
Mrs. E. W. Coxe, Red Oak, Iowa

On individual dishes arrange a little nest of the inner leaves of lettuce, and in the center of each nest, lay narrow strips of the white of hard boiled egg, placed in center. Rub the yolk of the egg through a colander and heap the yellow in the center with a spoonful of mayonnaise dressing.

PERFECTION SALAD
Mrs. G. W. Baxter

One-half package gelatine, one-half cup cold water, one-half cup vinegar, juice of one lemon, one pint boiling water, one-half cup sugar, one teaspoon salt, two cups celery in small pieces, one cup shredded cabbage, fine, one-fourth can sweet red peppers cut fine. Soak gelatine in cold water two minutes, add vinegar, lemon, water, sugar and salt; strain and add other ingredients. Mold and chill. Serve on lettuce leaves with mayonnaise dressing or cut in dice and serve in peppers.

BEET SALAD
Mrs. O. P. Johnston

One quart chopped beets (cooked), one head cabbage chopped fine, one cup grated horse raddish, one cup sugar, one cup vinegar, one teaspoon celery seed.

BEET SALAD
Anna M. Donley, Everist, Iowa

Select blood beets of uniform size, boil until tender, put in the ice box until needed, skin the beets and cut off a slice from the stem, remove the centers and fill with vinegar; when ready to serve, pour out the vinegar and fill full of chopped celery with a few broken English walnuts and mayonnaise dressing. Put on top of each a ring cut from hard boiled eggs. Sprinkle with bits of parsley.

POTATO SALAD
Mary E. Steele

Mince a small piece of onion in a chopping bowl. Add four boiled potatoes and whites of two hard-boiled eggs and chop fine. Season with salt and pepper. Mash the yolks of the eggs and one teaspoonful of butter to a paste, add very slowly enough vinegar to make a thin dressing, and pour over the potatoes, stirring very lightly. Just before serving add one gill of sweet cream.

OYSTER SALAD
Mrs. Josie Hobson, Albia

One can cove oysters, one-half pint rolled crackers, one-half pint vinegar, (if strong weaken), one-fourth pint butter, yolks of four eggs or two whole ones, one teaspoon salt, sugar and pepper to taste. Beat yolks, put crackers, liquor from oysters, butter and seasoning on stove, stir until it begins to thicken. Then add vinegar and eggs Cook until thick and pour over oysters.

POTATO SALAD
Mrs. Marie Vawter

Two cups celery, one-half gallon diced potatoes boiled in salt water, two onions. Dressing—yolks of two eggs, two tablespoons of sugar, one scant teaspoon mustard, one scant teaspoon celery seed, one scant teaspoon of salt, pepper and one-half pint vinegar.

East Side Public Square

GERMAN POTATO SALAD
Aimee Cornell

One dozen medium-sized potatoes boiled. While still warm skin potatoes and slice thin. Chop in a stalk of celery and a small onion. Season with handful of sugar, teaspoon of salt and dash of cayenne. Take a couple of slices of bacon and cut in small cubes. Put in skillet and brown, then pour in a pint of vinegar. Mix all these together. Garnish with parsley.

PEA SALAD
Mrs. H. L. Bousquet

One can French peas, same amount of ripe apples chopped, half amount of chopped celery. Serve with mayonnaise.

CUCUMBER SALAD
Flora Pitsor.

Pare and chop three medium sized cucumbers and as much again cabbage; mix and cover with any good mayonnaise dressing.

BEAN SALAD
Emily S. Cooper

One can red kidney beans, six sour pickles (rather large) three hard-boiled eggs, salt and pepper. Chop together and mix with dressing.

HOT SLAW
Edna Black

Chop fine one solid head cabbage. Put in stew kettle, add one cup water and let boil one hour and a half, adding more water sparingly. Then add pepper, one teaspoonful salt, one tablespoonful sugar and one cup vinegar. Let boil another hour, and before removing from kettle add one-half teaspoonful flour, let boil a few minutes and then remove.

CUCUMBER SALAD
Edna Black

Pare and slice fine six large cucumbers, sprinkle with a teaspoonful salt and let stand one-half hour. Press firmly and pour off all the juice. Then dress with pepper, teaspoonful sugar, one finely chopped onion, one-half cup thick sweet cream. While adding cream stir well to prevent curdling. Keep on ice till ready to serve.

RIPE TOMATO SALAD
Estella Wright

Pour boiling water over smooth tomatoes so as to remove the peeling, then chill them on ice; remove inside with paring knife and chop with equal parts of cabbage; salt and pepper to taste, mix with mayonnaise dressing and fill the cavity in the tomatoes with the mixture and serve on crisp lettuce.

CABBAGE SALAD
Mrs. M. D. Woodruff

Two tablespoons of whipped sweet cream, two tablespoons of sugar, four tablespoons of vinegar. Beat well and pour over cabbage, previously cut very fine, and season with salt.

COLD SLAW
Mrs. E. W. Coxe, Red Oak, Iowa

Three eggs, six tablespoons sweet cream, two tablespoons melted butter, one-half cup sugar, one level teaspoon pepper, one coffee cup vinegar; salt to taste. Let all simmer until it thickens. Thin with whipped or plain cream. This is sufficient for two quarts of finely shaved cabbage.

OYSTER SALAD
Mrs. J. V. Brann

One can cove oysters, one cup powdered crackers, one-half cup butter, three eggs, scant half cup vinegar, one teaspoon mustard, salt and pepper to taste. Drain off liquor and heat; stir in eggs, crackers and butter; let come to a boil and stir in vinegar and mustard. When it thickens pour over oysters. Garnish with parsley.

LOBSTER SALAD
Aimee Cornell

Chop one can lobsters and one stalk celery very fine, mix with mayonnaise dressing. Garnish with sliced lemon and parsley.

SALMON SALAD
Mrs. Louetta Hovey

One small can of salmon, one small bunch of celery, three hard boiled eggs. Chop fine and mix with mayonnaise dressing.

SALMON SALAD
Mrs. Louis Elliott

Flake one can of salmon and mix with minced parsley, celery and grated cucumber. Take one-half cupful boiled cream dressing, add one dessert spoonful of dissolved gelatine. Stir this into the dressing and set on ice until firm.

BOILED CREAM DRESSING FOR SALAD

One level teaspoon dry mustard, one heaping teaspoon salt, one level teaspoon sugar, one heaping tablespoon butter, one egg, one scant cup milk or cream, the cream either sweet or sour. Beat all together, cook until quite thick, add about one-third cup of hot vinegar. It should be the consistency of custard. If too thin thicken with corn starch. This makes one pint of dressing.

HAM SALAD

Mrs. J. H. Burma

Mince ham not very fine, add chopped egg and chopped lettuce. After arranging on lettuce leaves, place slices of hard boiled eggs on top. Add dressing.

DRESSING FOR SALAD

Beat three eggs until very stiff, add one cup sweet cream, one-half teaspoon salt. Mix thoroughly. Add one-half cup sharp vinegar, one-half teaspoon mustard, one-half cup melted butter, dessert spoon sugar. Beat again. Set bowl in kettle of hot water until dressing thickens. Mix mustard in a little vinegar to avoid lumps.

CHICKEN SALAD (One Chicken)

Mrs. Dickie C. Gebhardt

Boil the chicken until tender. Skin and pick to pieces (do not chop). Cut crisp celery into small bits. To one bowl of chicken use one bowl of celery. Dressing—Two eggs, four large tablespoons of vinegar, one tablespoon each of sugar and prepared mustard, one teaspoon yellow mustard, one-half teaspoon cornstarch, a little red pepper, a pinch of salt, butter size of an egg and one-half cup of thick, sweet cream. Beat yolks of eggs with sugar and cornstarch, add the red pepper, salt, vinegar and yellow mustard. Cook in double boiler till it thickens like float, then add butter. Take off the fire, then beat in prepared mustard and let cool. Just before you are ready for the salad beat the cream and white of eggs separate, then beat them together and beat into the cold dressing. Pour over chicken and celery, mixing thoroughly.

MUSHROOM SALAD
Edna Black

Take one cupful of any kind of left-over roast, diced. One can of mushrooms chopped fine, one grated onion and six sweet cucumber pickles chopped fine. Prepare with mayonnaise or French dressing.

CHICKEN SALAD
Mrs. Steele, Elkhart, Indiana

The white meat of two chickens cut up fine, and the same amount of celery. One pint of vinegar, four eggs, one teaspoonful salt, one-half teaspoonful pepper, two of melted butter and four of French mustard. Beat the eggs thoroughly and add the melted butter, salt, pepper and mustard, heat the vinegar to boiling point and pour in slowly, stirring constantly. Steam until it thickens. When thoroughly cold pour into the mixed chicken and celery.

BANANA SALAD
Mrs. Eugenia Hackley, Chicago, Illinois

Peel bananas and place on salad plates with curly lettuce. Use cream salad dressing and a generous supply of English walnut meats in halves on the dressing. Dressing—Yellow of six eggs, beat to a cream. Place on stove in a double boiler and add for each yellow one level tablespoon of vinegar. The vinegar should be added slowly to prevent curdling. When this has cooked until very stiff, take from the stove and while hot rub in a large tablespoon of butter. When cold beat in such condiments as are needed for the dish to be served. If the dressing is for fruit, less mustard and pepper should be used than for vegetables. But a small spoonful of sugar and half as much salt, a sprinkle of white pepper and pinch of mustard makes a very mild, rich dressing. Beat thoroughly and add half a cup of whipped cream just before serving.

FRUIT SALAD
Mrs. T. G. Gilson

Put one cupful of cold water over one package of gelatine, soak one hour. Add two coffee cups boiling water and one cup of sugar. Mix well and let cool. One can pineapple cut in small pieces, four oranges shredded and cut up fine, one dozen fresh or one can of peaches cut fine, one-half pound English walnuts. Candied cherries and most any fruit can be added. Mix all together and set in a cool place. Twice this amount will serve seventy-five.

FRUIT SALAD
Laura Parsons

One package Jello, three oranges, three bananas, two small cans pineapple, one large bottle cock-tail cherries, one small cup English walnuts cut fine. Cut fruit in very small pieces, add part of juice and cup and half of sugar. Makes one-half gallon.

WHITE GRAPE SALAD
Mrs. R. G. Emmel, Harvey, Iowa

One pound white grapes, skin, cut in two and remove seeds; one cup celery, one cup chopped nuts, one small bottle Maraschino cherries, with following mayonnaise dressing: Yolks of two eggs, juice of one lemon, half teaspoon dry mustard. Mix thoroughly. Add by degrees in small quantities one tablespoon vinegar, then one-half pint salad oil, only a few drops at a time, stirring rapidly all the time, salt and a little pepper. A boiled dressing may be used for this salad as well as the oil dressing.

WHITE CHERRY SALAD
Mrs. R. S. Granger, Eureka Springs, Arkansas

One can of white cherries seeded, one-half pound of blanched almonds, one pint chopped celery. Pour over mayonnaise dressing and serve.

EXCELLENT SALAD AND DRESSING
Mrs. Mell Woodruff

Three cups of celery chopped fine, one cup tart apples, one cup pineapple or white grapes, one cup nuts and a few cherries. Add mayonnaise dressing until right consistency. Dressing—Yolks of eight eggs beaten light, eight tablespoons vinegar, butter size of egg. Scald vinegar and pour over yolks, stir well and return to kettle, stir until it thickens like custard. Take from fire and stir in butter. Let it get perfectly cold. Take two parts of dressing to one part whipped cream. Before adding cream put one teaspoon dry mustard. Use salt and cayenne pepper to taste. Two tablespoons sugar or less, as you wish it sweet or sour.

PINEAPPLE AND CELERY SALAD
Mrs. Dell McDonald, Des Moines, Iowa

To two cups shredded pineapple add one cup of chopped celery and one sweet red pepper cut into dice. For the dressing use a mayonnaise cream dressing, which is the ordinary mayonnaise slightly reduced with whipped cream. Serve very cold on lettuce hearts garnished with nut meats, or it may be served in cups make of apples peeled and scooped out, or it may be packed in a ring mould, turned out on a platter, the center piled with lettuce hearts and a few arranged around the ring.

CELERY AND NUT SALAD
Mrs. Maggie Roberts

Remove the shells from about two dozen English walnuts, turn boiling water over the meats and let them stand fifteen minutes, then drain, remove the skins and break into small pieces. Cut an equal quantity of celery into small pieces, mix with nuts, heap in crisp lettuce cups, dress with mayonnaise and garnish with whole walnut meats.

APPLE SALAD
Mrs. A. B. Culver

Chop six apples, one bunch celery, one cup English walnuts. Pour mayonnaise dressing over all and mix thoroughly.

MAYONAISE DRESSING
Mrs. Louetta Hovey

Two eggs, one cup of cream (sweet), one-third cup of sugar, one-half cup of vinegar, one level teaspoon of mustard, one level teaspoon celery seed, salt and pepper, butter size of a walnut. Mix all together and let come to a boil.

FRENCH SALAD DRESSING
Belle Collins-Jacob, New York City

This dressing is good with green salads. One table-spoon of lemon juice to three of pure olive oil or salad oil, one-half teaspoon of salt, one-quarter teaspoon of pepper. Mix the salt and pepper with the oil, then stir in slowly the lemon juice. It should be blended so as to taste of neither the oil nor the lemon juice.

COOKED SALAD DRESSING
Mrs. W. S. Bilby

Bring to a boil one cup vinegar. Beat the yolks of six eggs thoroughly with one tablespoon of cold vinegar. Pour this mixture into the boiling vinegar and set on stove until it thickens. After removing from stove add one-fourth pound butter. When cold add as much whipped cream as there is dressing. Season to taste with salt, mustard, red and black pepper which have previously been mixed.

WALDORF SALAD
Mrs. Della Myers

One cup apples cut in cubes, one cup celery, one-half cup English walnuts. Serve on lettuce with salad dressing. Garnish with half walnuts.

The Parsons Hotel

BREAD

ROLLS, BISCUITS, MUFFINS, ETC.

"Light, crisp rolls for breakfast; spongy, sweet bread for dinner, and flaky biscuits for supper, cover a multitude of culinary sins."

NEW WOMEN'S YEAST

Mrs. Anna Long

Three large potatoes, boil in one quart water; scald one cup flour, one tablespoon sugar, one teaspoon salt. Beat till very light. Also beat the potatoes and add to this. Add cold water to make in all one half gallon. Add one yeast cake. Let stand until it works well and settles. Put away in separate jars so as not to disturb the balance. Use this with half water to make bread. Be sure to salt your bread. Bread may be made stiff with this yeast without sponging. Will keep several weeks in cool place.

BREAD

Mrs. Marie Vawter

Take one cake of good yeast. Dissolve in one cup of warm water, add enough flour to make stiff enough to drop from spoon. Set aside in warm place. Do this when getting supper. Scald a good quart of buttermilk, set aside and skim, drain and add one pint lukewarm water. Now add flour enough to make quite stiff sponge. Beat well then add yeast. Set in warm place over night. Next morning add one tablespoon lard, two of sugar, one of salt, add enough flour to make stiff. Set in warm place to rise. Let rise and work down and let rise again, mould into loaves and bake.

JUG YEAST

Mrs. Dell McDonald, Des Moines

Boil one handful of hops in a quart of water. Boil twelve good sized potatoes in the least water practicable. Strain the hop water on the potatoes, add a teacup of sugar a tablespoon of ginger, a tablespoon of salt. Mash all together. When lukewarm add a teacup of yeast and set in warm place to rise. The special point to this yeast is there is no flour in it.

BROWN BREAD

Miss Josie Hobson, Albia Iowa

Two cups sour milk, two cups graham flour, 1 cup wheat flour, one-half cup molasses, (sorghum best) one tablespoon sugar, two teaspoons (even) of soda, one teaspoon salt, one cup raisins. Mix, pour into greased pan and raise one hour. Put in oven and bake one hour.

WHITE BREAD

Northwestern Yeast Co.

One pint water drained from boiled potatoes, with two tablespoonful finely mashed potatoes added. Set it aside and scald a pint of milk, adding, when scalded, one tablespoon sugar and one teaspoon salt. Now in a quart bowl put a teacup of lukewarm water and one cake of YEAST FOAM. Let it dissolve slowly, then add a pinch of salt and enough flour to thicken moderately. Place it where it will keep warm, and at night put the potato water, milk and risen Yeast together in the bread bowl, stirring in enough flower to make a stiff batter; beat well and set it where it will keep warm. In the morning stir in one-half teaspoon soda dissolved in warm water, add flour to mould stiff, let it rise again and make it into loaves.

YEAST AND BREAD
Lute Parsons.

Six good sized Irish potatoes boiled in two quarts of water. When done pour off the water and keep hot. Mash the potatoes, sift over them one pint flour, then add the hot potato water and enough cold water to make a gallon, then add two and one-half cakes of yeast.

Bread—For three loaves—One large tablespoon of lard and one of sugar, teaspoon of salt, one tin cupful of hot water to disolve this, and same amount of cold water and enough flour to make a stiff batter. One tin cup of yeast, then pour this batter into the flour and mix it up pretty stiff and let it raise for the first time. Knead down once and then after raising put in pans, let raise and bake.

WHOLE WHEAT BREAD (OR GRAHAM)
Mrs. Anna Long.

One pint white bread sponge, one-half pint warm water, one-half tablespoon lard, one tablespoon sugar, salt to taste. Make soft dough, let rise once very light. Put in pans, let get quite light; bake as other bread. When taken out of oven grease top well with butter to soften crust. If desired a piece of white dough may be kneaded out the length of the loaf and placed in the middle of the loaf, making a white spot in each slice. If all whole wheat is desired set the sponge of whole wheat.

CORN BREAD
Ella McClure

One-half pint finely-bolted corn meal, one-half pint flour, one tablespoon sugar, one teaspoon salt, two teaspoons baking powder; mix well while dry, then add two well beaten eggs and milk or milk and water to make a moderately thin batter. Bake in shallow, well buttered pans.

GRAHAM BREAD
Mrs. A. T. Looney.

Sponge one yeast cake at noon. At night add three cups of lukewarm water and set with flour as for white bread. In the morning, when very light, add three cups of lukewarm water, one cup of molasses, one cup of sugar, small handful of salt, three tablespoons of melted lard, three pints of graham flour and stiffen with white flour. Knead well. When it has raised knead again and shape into loaves. When they have raised work them again and when light bake in a slow oven for one and one-fourth hours.

SALT RISING BREAD
Mrs. Kellum.

Take one and one-half cupful warm water, half cup milk a teaspoon of salt, half teaspoon salaratus, put in a tin pail that will cover tight, then put in flour enough to make a batter, set in a kettle on back of stove about five hours. Sift in bread bowl as much fiour as you wish, make a hole in center, put in a pint of warm water, stir to a batter, taking the flour from the sides and add the yeast. When risen, mix and form in loaves, let it rise again and bake in moderate oven about half an hour.

STIRRED BREAD
Mrs. Ralph Proudfit, Chariton, Iowa

One quart tepid water, one cake compressed yeast, two tablespoons sugar, two tablespoons melted butter, one teaspoon salt. Stir in five pints flour and let stand over night. In the morning stir down well and let rise a second time; stir down with a silver knife or spoon and turn into small buttered pans. The yeast should be soaked in a little warm water for a few minutes. This bread is not touched with the hands and does not require kneading.

STEAMED CORN BREAD

Mrs. Charles Fagan, Ft, Madison, Iowa

One egg, three-fourths cup molasses, two cups of sweet milk, one cup butter, one cup flour, three cups corn meal, one tablespoon melted butter, one teaspoon soda, one-half teaspoon salt. Steam three hours.

NUT BREAD

Edna Black

Three and one-half cups flour, (part pastry), one teaspoon salt, three and one-half teaspoons baking powder, one cup sugar, all sifted together four or five times, one egg beaten, one cup milk, 1 cup rolled nuts (any kind). Let raise twenty minutes, bake in slow oven one hour or a little over. The success of this bread is in the baking.

CORN BREAD

Stella W. Wright

One and three-fourth pints corn meal, one-fourth pint flour (scant), one pint sour milk, two eggs beaten very light, one-half teacup sugar, piece of butter the size of an egg, add the last thing one teaspoon soda in a little milk. Add to the beaten eggs the milk and meal alternately, then the butter and sugar and soda. Bake twenty minutes.

CORN BREAD

Mrs. T. G. Gilson

Make mush with one cup of corn meal and boiling water, add some salt, let cool, then add one tablespoon butter and one tablespoon sugar, two eggs well beaten, two-thirds cup flour in which mix one large teaspoon of baking powder and two-thirds of a cup of corn meal, Beat well and bake.

CORN BREAD
Mrs. H. A. Shirer.

One pint corn meal, one pint flour, small tablespoon sugar, pinch of salt, two teaspoonsful baking powder, tablespoon shortening, stir and mix with water.

BOSTON BROWN BREAD
Mrs. A. B. Brobst

Two cups of corn meal, one cup of graham flour, two cups of sour milk, two-thirds cup of molasses, one teaspoon of salt, two teaspoons soda dissolved in one-half cup hot water. Steam two hours and bake thirty minutes.

BROWN BREAD
Miss Belle Pollock, Los Angeles, Cal.

Two and one-half cups of graham flour, one-half cup corn meal, one cup of white flour, one cup of sweet milk, one cup of New Orleans molasses, one cup sour milk, one egg, one teaspoon of soda dissolved in a little hot water. Add one cup of raisins rolled in flour; a little salt. Steam three hours.

OATMEAL BREAD
Eva Belville

Take two and one-half cups well boiled oat meal porridge, cold; add one-half cup molasses, one-half cup liquid yeast or one-half yeast cake, one tablespoon salt, and knead in enough wheat flour to make the consistency of ordinary bread dough. Mould into loaves, put in baking pans, let raise very light and bake an hour and a half. The lightness and long baking are very necessary to success. The bread is better a little stale than when fresh.

PARKER HOUSE ROLLS

Mrs. Marie Vawter

Rub one-half tablespoon of butter and one-half table-spoon lard into two quarts sifted flour. Into a well in the middle pour one pint cold boiled milk and add one-half cup of yeast (or one yeast cake), one-half cup sugar and a little salt. If wanted for tea, rub the flour and butter, boil and cool the milk the night before, add sugar, yeast and salt and turn all into the flour, but do not stir. Let stand over night and in the morning stir up. Knead and let rise till near tea time. Mold and let rise again and bake quickly. To mold, cut with cake cutter, put a little melted butter on one-half and lap nearly over on the other half, place in pan about three-fourths of an inch apart.

BUNS

Mrs. S. D. McClelland

Half a cake of yeast well soaked, add to one pint of warm water stirred stiff with flour, make in evening, Next morning add one pint warm water, one cup lard, three-fourths cup of sugar, one tablespoon salt. Mix same as for bread. Let rise all day, mix down once. Butter the hands and make out in balls about the size of an egg, place far apart in buttered pan. If for supper, make out in the morning, if for breakfast make out in evening. Bake fifteen minutes. Keep remainder of dough in a cool place. Will make fifty buns.

CINNAMON ROLLS

Mary E. Steele

Take lump of raised dough size of loaf, roll thin, spread with butter, sugar and cinnamon and roll as for jelly cake; cut into slices one inch thick and place in pans; let rise until light, and bake.

ROLLS
Mrs. W. S. Bilby

One cup scalded sweet milk, one-fourth cup sugar, one-fourth cup melted butter, two well beaten eggs, one cup light sponge, one pinch nutmeg, three and one-half cups flour, salt. When milk is luke warm add two cups flour and sponge. Beat well and let rise, then add butter, sugar and salt, nutmeg and eggs. Add flour to make a soft dough. Knead well, let rise again. Shape into small rolls. Let rise in buttered pans and bake in moderate oven.

BAKING POWDER BISCUIT
Mrs. C. A. Reaver, Eldora, Iowa

Two cups of flour, one-half teaspoon of salt, two teaspoons baking powder, one teaspoon shortening to each cup of flour, three-fourths cup of milk. Flour the board well. Never fails.

CINNAMON ROLLS
Florence Gamble

A piece of light bread dough about the size of a loaf. To this add one egg, one tablespoon of butter, one-half cup of milk, one cup of sugar, one tablespoon of cinnamon, work thoroughly, make into rolls and set to rise. When almost done spread with a mixture of three tablespoons of butter, one of sugar and one of cinnamon,

GERMAN COFFEE CAKE
Bertha S. Black

Use same sponge as for rusks, adding a cup of seeded raisins. put thin layer into buttered cake tins; let rise, brush with butter, sprinkle thickly with sugar and ground almonds, also with thick cream, and bake in a moderate oven.

Residence of O. P. Wright

BAKING POWDER BISCUIT
Mrs. Mollie Mentzer

Three cups of flour, three teaspoons baking powder, one-half teaspoon salt. Sift well together and to this add lard and butter size of an egg. Mix well into flour (as for pie crust). Pour in enough rich milk to make soft dough; mix with fork, turn out on bread board and shape with the hand. Use small biscuit cutter and bake in quick oven.

SODA BISCUIT
Mrs. R. J. Casteel

Rub into a quart of sifted flour a piece of butter the size of an egg, one teaspoon of salt, stir into this a pint of sour milk, dissolve one teaspoon of soda and stir into the milk just as you add it to the flour; knead up quickly, roll out nearly half an inch thick and cut out with a biscuit cutter; bake immediately in a quick oven. Very nice biscuit may be made with thick, sour cream without the butter by the same process.

SPICED CAKE
Mrs. Elsie Worstell

Two cups bread sponge, three eggs, one level teaspoon soda, one-half cup raisins, one heaping cup sugar, one cup of flour, three-fourths cup shortening, one teaspoon cloves, one teaspoon cinnamon. Bake in a moderate oven three-fourths of an hour. Cover with a thin icing.

RAISED CAKE
Mrs. Joe Johnston

Two cups raised dough, two cups sugar, one cup butter, one cup sweet milk, two cups flour, two eggs, one teaspoon soda, one cup raisins (seeded), two teaspoons ground cinnamon, one teaspoon ground cloves, one teaspoon ground ginger.

GERMAN RUSK
Bertha Black

Soak two cakes of yeast in luke warm water in the morning. Add flour to make a thick batter and set in a warm place till evening. Then take one quart of warm milk, one cup of sugar, one teaspoon of salt, one cup butter, three well beaten eggs; add all to the milk and stir in enough flour to make a stiff dough. Add yeast and let rise over night. Beat light in the morning, let rise again and mold into rusks size of a walnut. Let these rise, brush butter over top and bake in a moderate oven fifteen minutes.

MUFFINS For Two
Mrs. J. H. Burma

Beat one small egg until light, one-half cup milk, salt spoon of salt, two-thirds of a cup of flour. Beat well. Add level teaspoon baking powder. Bake in quick oven fifteen minutes.

MUFFINS
Nan Cornell

One egg beaten light with one cup of milk, one table spoon of lard, two and one-half cups flour with two large teaspoons of baking powder sifted with flour.

CORN MUFFINS
Mrs C. M. Harrington

One cup corn meal, two cups flour, two cups sweet milk, one-half cup sugar, one-third cup butter, little salt, two teaspoons baking powder. Bake in muffin rings or gem pans.

GRAHAM GEMS
Mrs. Delia Brobst

One pint of buttermilk, with a level teaspoon soda, two cups graham flour, one-third cup of sugar, one egg, salt; bake in quick oven.

WHEAT GEMS
Mrs. Lura Hanks

One cup milk, one-half teaspoon salt, one heaping teaspoon baking powder, enough flour to make a stiff batter, two tablespoons melted butter, stirred in last. Drop in hot gem pans and bake quickly.

COCOA GEMS
Miss Lucia Jenkins

One-fourth cup batter, one-fourth cup cocoa, one-fourth cup of sugar, three-fourths cup milk, one and one-half cups flour, one egg, two teaspoons baking powder. Cream the butter and sugar; add the well beaten egg, then milk; sift the flour, cocoa and baking powder together thoroughly and add; bake fifteen minutes. This recipe makes eight gems. Dainty to serve with tea or coffee for lunch.

POP OVERS
Blanche Elliott

One cup flour, two teaspoons baking powder, one cup milk, one egg, one teaspoon melted butter, pinch salt; bake in gem pans fifteen or twenty minutes.

NAGASAKI BISCUIT
Nora Neal

One pint of bread sponge, one-half cup (small) sugar, butter size of walnut; mix these thoroughly, then add flour until almost as stiff as bread dough; let rise, then handle as little as possible, rolling it about one inch thick; spread with butter, sprinkle with sugar, commence at side and roll light and cut in rounds about one inch thick; place in a pan as biscuit, close together, let rise quite light, then bake,

Sponge Cake   Mrs. Johnson

1 cup light sponge   ½ cup butter
1 ...   1 cup raisens or currents.
1 teaspoon soda 1 egg about one cup flour
all kind of spices.

Pineapple ~~Cake~~

1¼ cup sugar.   scant ¾ cup butter.
½ 2 p pineapple juice fill cup with
water 2½ cups flour before sifting
3 teaspoons B. P.   Warm sugar +
cream with butter, add flour and
moisture gardually , then whites of 4
eggs.
          Filling
1 white g egg not beaten 1tablespoon lemon
juice ¼ cup grated pineapple.
Beat in powered sugar about 2 cups
until stiffened.
          Apples r peaches can be used.

Dolly Varden Cake.

Dark Part

½ cup butter ⅓ cup milk
2½ cups flour 1 cup sugar
½ cup syrup yolks of four eggs.
2 teaspoon B. P. 1 cup raisins ½ currents
1 teaspoon cloves, cinnamon ½ nutmeg.

Light Part.

whites of 3 eggs 1 cup milk.
1½ cups sugar ½ cup butter
2½ cups flour 2 teaspoons B. P.
2 teaspoons vanilla.

Graham Pudding.

1 cup mollasses 1 cup sour milk
1 cup fruit
1 teaspoon salt 2 cups Graham flour
½ teaspoon cloves 1 teaspoon soda.
1 teaspoon cinnamon
steam 2 hrs, then put in oven ½ hr.

Yellow Corn meal Muffins.

2 tablespoons butter

1 egg

2/3 cup flour

2 teaspoons B. P.

2 tablespoons sugar

1 cup milk

1 cup corn meal

Muffins

1 tablespoon butter

2 cups flour

1 cup milk

2 tablespoons sugar

2 teaspoons B. P.

2 eggs.

Penochee (Mexican candy)
2 cups light brown sugar 1 cup milk
10 cts English walnuts ground or chopped
butter size of a small egg. 1
teaspon lemon. cook same as
fudge stir after removing from
fire.

GRIDDLE CAKES, FRITTERS, AND WAFFLES

RICE GRIDDLE CAKES

From the Rice Kitchen, Louisiana Purchase Exposition

Two cups rice, two cups flour, two cups milk, one-half teaspoon salt, two eggs, three level teaspoons baking powder. Stir the salt and milk in cooked rice and add the well-beaten yolks of eggs, and the sifted flour and baking powder; lastly the stiffly beaten whites of eggs. Bake on a hot griddle.

RICE GRIDDLE CAKES

Nora Elliott

Mash one cup cooked rice, add one beaten egg and one and one-half cups sweet milk. Sift one and one-half level teaspoons baking powder with one cup sifted pastry flour; a pinch of salt; stir into mixture. If not thick enough add a little more flour very cautiously. Bake on griddle, using but one tablespoonful for each cake.

CORN FRITTERS

Mrs. C C. Cunningham

One pint grated corn, two eggs, one-half-cup butter; season highly with salt and pepper and fry in butter.

SHELBY'S GRIDDLE CAKES

One pint Shelby's Self Rising Health Flour, one scant pint milk or water. Bake on hot griddle.

First Methodist Episcopal Church

BUCKWHEAT CAKES
Chicago Daily News Cook Book

Buckwheat cakes once tested from the following no other will be used. Two cupsful buckwheat, one cupful graham, half teaspoon salt, one large teaspoon baking powder, all sifted together. Mix with milk into a thin batter. Bake on a hot griddle and serve immediately.

YEAST BUCKWHEAT CAKES
Mrs. Edith Ogle

One pint buckwheat flour, one-half pint wheat flour, one teaspoon salt. At noon scald with potato water or hot water three heaping tablespoons flour. When cool add one cake soaked yeast and let stand until bedtime. Then add four tablespoons yeast to the buckwheat flour, and enough warm water to make batter. Let stand until morning, add pinch of soda and bake. Stand balance of yeast in cool place, add one tablespoon of mixed flour to batter each night.

CORN MEAL GRIDDLE CAKES
Prue W. Collins

One pint sour cream or milk, one teaspoon soda, salt, yolk of 1 egg, equal parts corn meal and flour to make batter. Stir well all ingredients. Add last the white of egg well beaten.

BATTER CAKES
Tested

One pint of sweet milk, generous pinch of salt, whites of two eggs and one large teaspoon baking powder. Stir salt in milk, add flour till you have a pretty stiff batter, next stir in baking powder and add well beaten whites of eggs the last thing, mixing the whole gently.

BREAD GRIDDLE CAKES
By Request

One quart milk boiling hot, two cups fine bread crumbs, three eggs, one tablespoon lard or melted butter, one-half teaspoon salt, one-half teaspoon soda dissolved in a little warm water. Put bread crumbs into boiling milk and let stand for ten minutes in a covered bowl, then beat into a smooth paste, add yolks of eggs well whipped, the butter, salt, soda and finally whites of eggs whipped stiff and add half cup flour. These can be made of sour milk, soaking milk and bread over night and using a little more soda.

GRIDDLE CAKES
Mrs. S. C. Johnston

One cup of flour, two tablespoons of corn meal, two rounding teaspoons of baking powder, salt to taste. Mix to a smooth batter with sweet milk. Add one well beaten egg.

RECIPE FOR MAKING ROSETTE WAFERS
Mrs. C. W. Bellville

Take—two eggs, one teaspoon of sugar, one-fourth teaspoon of salt, one cup of milk, one cup of flour (a little more if necessary.) Beat eggs slightly with sugar and salt, add milk and flour, beat until smooth. This amount will make forty rosettes. Screw handle into one of the irons and put Rosette Iron in hot lard or oil to heat before dipping it into the batter, not letting the batter come over the top of the iron. Return it to the hot lard, thoroughly covering the iron with same, for at least twenty seconds, but not over thirty-five seconds. If wanted for oyster patties, or instead of toast, leave the sugar out of the batter.

COCOANUT FRITTERS

Tested

One cup of grated cocoanut, one cup of flour, one-fourth teaspoon salt, one teaspoon sugar, scant teaspoon baking powder, one egg, one tablespoon melted butter, one teaspoon vanilla and sufficient milk to make a thick batter. This is dropped by spoonfuls into hot, smoking fat and cooked a golden brown. After draining, the fritters may be rolled in powdered sugar. Serve immeiately.

APPLE FRITTERS

Mary Anthes

Make a light batter of three eggs, one cup sour cream, a little soda and salt, flour to thicken. Take a half dozen ripe apples, pare and chop fine, stir them in the batter, also a heaping tablespoon of sugar. Have a frying pan of hot lard, drop the mixture by spoonfuls, fry light brown. Sprinkle with white sugar as they are taken up.

BANANA FRITTERS

Congregational Cook Book

Make a batter in the proportion of one cup sweet milk to two cups flour, a heaping teaspoon baking powder, two eggs well beaten, one tablespoon sugar, a pinch of salt. Heat the milk a little more than milk warm and add slowly to beaten eggs and sugar. Then add the flour, stir all together and drop in pieces of banana cut about an inch long, dipping the batter up over them. Drop in boiling hot lard in large spoonfuls and fry to a light brown. Serve with maple syrup or with a syrup made of light brown sugar.

DELICIOUS FRITTERS
Mary Anthes

Take one quart of water, and a piece of butter the size of a hen's egg,boil a few minutes,then stir in enough flour to make as thick as mashed potatoes. Pour this into a bowl and beat six eggs in it, one at a time, add a little salt and nutmeg, then fry in hot lard.

WAFFLES
Mrs. C. C. C.

To one pint of flour add one pint of sour milk, two eggs well beaten, two tablespoons sugar, two tablespoons melted butter or lard, one saltspoon salt. Just before baking add one level teaspoon soda dissolved in hot water. Bake in very hot waffle irons.

WAFFLES
Alice Bellamy

Four eggs, one quart flour, one quart milk (sweet), butter or lard size of an egg, two teaspoons baking powder, one teaspoon salt. Beat yolks very light, add milk, then the flour with the baking powder and salt sifted with it, then the melted lard or butter, and last the well beaten whites.

SWEET WAFFLES
Mrs. C. C. Cnnningham.

One tea cup butter, two teacups sugar, three cups flour and four eggs. Flavor with nutmeg and bake in waffle irons.

PUDDINGS AND SAUCES

"You dressing, dancing, gadding, where's the good in,
Sweet lady, tell me, can you make a pudding?"

PLUM PUDDING
Mrs. M. A. Wright

One cup suet chopped fine, two cups fine bread crumbs, one heaping cup sugar, one cup seeded raisins, one cup washed currants, one cup almonds, one-half cup citron, one teaspoon salt, one teaspoon cloves, two teaspoons cinnamon, half nutmeg, four beaten eggs, one teaspoon soda, cup milk, pint flour. Chop fruit and almonds and put over them the flour. Put eggs, sugar, spices, salt and milk in a bowl. Stir in fruit, nuts, bread and suet. Lastly add soda dissolved in one tablespoon warm water. Steam four hours.

BAKED ENGLISH PLUM PUDDING
Alice Bellamy

Six eggs beaten together, one coffee cup brown sugar, three pints new milk, one pound bread crumbs, one-fourth pound suet chopped fine, one pound raisins, one half pound currants, one-fourth pound citron, two tablespoons cinnamon, one teaspoon cloves, grated peel one lemon. Mix all together and bake three hours in slow oven. This pudding is better when made the day before it is used, and then steamed until hot. Serve with the following sauce: Two cups of sugar, one cup butter, one teaspoon vanilla. Beat until very light and grate nutmeg over it.

PEACH PUDDING
Ruby Gamble

Peel some nice peaches, fill dish half full, nearly cover with water, add a half cup of sugar; make a crust of one pint of flour, one heaping teaspoon of baking powder, butter the size of an egg, mix with water, roll out the dough, and cover the peaches; cover with dish the same size. May be cooked on top of stove or in the oven. Cook until peaches are done and serve with sugar and cream. (Excellent)

PEACH ROLL
By Request

Make crust the same as for baking powder biscuit; roll very thin, a little longer than wide, spread with butter, then spread with stewed dried peaches which are mashed fine and sweetened, and drained free from juice; roll and place in a thin cloth which has been thoroughly wet, allowing plenty of room for pudding to expand; then place in a colander and set over boiling water to steam. When done cut in slices and serve with a sauce prepared from creaming one-half cup of butter, gradually adding one and one-half cups of light brown sugar. Beat until consistency of thick cream. This is fine.

SUET PUDDING
Mrs. J. W. Avery

One cup suet chopped fine, one cup sugar, one of currants, one of raisins, two of flour, two eggs, one teaspoon of salt, one and one-half cups Malta Vita or bread crumbs, one cup of sour milk, one teaspoon of soda, one of cinnamon, one of allspice, one of nutmeg and one-half of cloves. Boil in cloth two hours.

SAUCE

One cup of sugar, butter size of an egg, one and one-half cups of water. Thicken with flour and flavor with vanilla. Serve warm.

COTTAGE PUDDING FOR QUICK DINNER
Mrs. P. M. Stentz

Three-fourths cup sugar, two cups flour, one cup of sweet milk, one egg, one tablespoon butter, two teaspoons baking powder. Sift flour and baking powder, cream butter and sugar, add the yolks of eggs, well beaten, then the milk. Stir in the flour and add the white of egg, beaten very stiff. Serve hot with liquid sauce.

COTTAGE PUDDING
Ella Kinne

One cup sugar, one-half cup butter, one egg, cup of sweet milk, one teaspoon soda dissolved in milk and two teaspoons cream tartar in three scant cups of flour; one-half teaspoon extract of lemon; sprinkle a little sugar over the top before putting in the oven; bake in a long bread pan (fifteen inches). Cut in squares and serve with sliced bananas and sweetened cream. What is left from dinner may be served for tea.

CHOCOLATE PUDDING
Mrs. A. B. Culver

Yolks of three eggs, one scant cup sugar, thirteen tablespoons rolled crackers, six tablespoons grated chocolate, one quart boiling milk in which the chocolate has been dissolved. Beat the sugar and eggs, add slowly the milk, then the crackers. Cook until thick; beat the whites of three eggs, adding one small tablespoon of sugar to each egg. Put on top and set in oven to brown. Serve with cream or sauce.

SAUCE

One cup sugar, two tablespoons flour, two tablespoons butter, mixed with a little cold water. Pour on a pint of boiling water and cook until thick. Flavor.

PUDDING
Mrs. Jessie Bilby

Use batter as given for cherry puffs, put in pudding dish and stir in cherries, sliced apples, sliced or canned peaches or berries and steam for an hour. Serve with cream and sugar or pudding sauce. This makes a splendid easy pudding.

RAISIN PUDDING
Mrs. Della Myers

Three eggs, one-half cup butter, one cup sour cream, one even teaspoon soda, one cup sugar, one cup raisins, and enough flour to make batter like cake dough. Bake in moderate oven. Serve with cream or hot sauce.

CHOCOLATE PUDDING
Emily S. Cooper

One quart sweet milk, one small cup sugar, two tablespoons grated chocolate. Heat and thicken with one egg and two tablespoons corn starch, moistened with milk. Pour into moulds and let cool. Serve with cream.

CHOCOLATE BREAD PUDDING
Anna M. Donley, Everist, Iowa

One pint stale bread crushed fine, one quart milk, two eggs, one saltspoon salt, one saltspoon ground cinnamon, three tablespoons sugar, two ounces chocolate grated; mix together, adding beaten eggs last; form in buttered pudding dish and bake until nice brown. It is nice served with egg sauce.

EGG SAUCE

Beat whites of eggs to stiff froth, beat into this slowly only one cup of powdered sugar, one teaspoon vanilla, two eggs, yolks only; beat the mixture a minute longer, then stir in one cup of whipped cream or three tablespoons of milk; serve at once.

Residence of J. B. Elliott

CHOCOLATE RICE PUDDING

Mrs. Maude Mentzer

Scald two cups milk, add one-fourth cup uncooked rice, one-half teaspoon salt and cook until nice and tender; one tablespoon butter, one-third cup sugar, one square Baker's chocolate melted, one-half teaspoon vanilla, one-half cup chopped almonds, one half cup seeded raisins, cut and fold in the whites of two eggs and one half cup whipped cream; pour mixture into a buttered pudding dish; bake twenty minutes, spread with meringue of whites of three eggs, one-half cup powdered sugar, one-half teaspoon vanilla, browned.

RICE PUDDING

Mrs. J. A. J. Powers

Three tablespoons rice, four tablespoons of sugar, butter size of an egg and one teaspoon of vanilla. Grate nutmeg over top and fill pudding dish with good sweet milk. Bake in moderate oven for two hours. As milk cooks away refill until you have a thick, creamy pudding. Soak rice over night.

SOFT PUDDING

Mrs. W. C. Mentzer

Into two-well-beaten eggs stir two teaspoons of sugar, one cup milk, one-half cup melted butter, two cups flour containing three teaspoons baking powder, one cup of any kind of cooked fruit—jam is best. Steam in individual moulds for twenty-five minutes, and serve with following sauce: One-half cup sugar mixed well with one tablespoon corn starch. Pour in one cup boiling water, two tablespoons lemon juice, four tablespoons of butter. Cook until thick and color with fruit coloring.

STEAMED PUDDING
Willa Underhill

One-half-cup molasses, one-fourth cup butter, one egg, one-half cup sour milk, one-half teaspoon soda, one and a half cups graham flour, one teacup raisins, one-half cup currants, spice to taste. Steam four hours. Serve with sauce,

LEMON SNOW PUDDING
Blanche Elliott

Two cups hot water, one cup sugar, two tablespoons corn starch, juice of two lemons. Boil two minutes, beat whites of four eggs and stir in.

DRESSING

Yolks of four eggs to one quart of milk, sweeten and flavor to taste. Very nice served in sherbet cups. Half of recipe will serve six people.

BLACK PUDDING
Mrs. Geo. P Anthes

Three eggs, one cup of sugar, one cup of jam, one teaspoon soda in one-half cup buttermilk, one cup of flour; beat whites and yellows separately, using yellows for meringue; bake pudding, then add meringue and brown that. Serve with hot sauce.

SALLY LUNN
Mrs. Kate Wilson

One cup of sugar well beaten with two eggs, one cup of milk, one and one-half cups of flour, two tablespoons of baking powder; stir briskly and put in a buttered pan and bake in quick oven. Serve warm with hard sauce.

LEMON PUDDING

Anna M. Donley, Everist, Iowa.

Batter—one-half cup sugar, one tablespoon butter, one egg, one-half cup milk, one-half cup flour, two teaspoons baking powder. Syrup—one large lemon sliced fine, one cup sugar, one tablespoon butter, two cups water; boil until lemon is cooked; put in buttered pan, pour syrup over and bake. It is nice served with whipped cream.

SAGO PUDDING

Mrs. Myrtle Orcutt

Two-thirds cup sago; cook until done; have it about as thick as mush to fry; add the stiffly beaten whites of two eggs and sugar to taste; put in dish to cool; put cherries or raspberries on top and whipped cream on that.

EXCELLENT PUDDING

Ella McClure

One and one-half pints of milk, two eggs and a small tablespoon of flour. Mix flour with milk to the consistency of thick cream; boil rest of milk and pour boiling hot upon flour, stirring all the time; add little salt, sugar, to taste and when cold, two eggs well beaten. Have ready a buttered dish and pour the whole into it; grate lemon peel or nutmeg over it and bake fifteen minutes.

CHERRY PUFFS

Mrs. Kate Wilson

One egg, well beaten, one-half cup milk, butter size of a walnut, one cup of flour, one teaspoon of baking powder. Drop a tablespoon into a buttered cup and into this put two tablespoons of cherries, canned or fresh, then more batter. Steam thirty minutes. This will make four or five puffs. Serve with sauce or cream and sugar.

APPLE PUDDING
Mrs. C. C. Cunningham

One-half cup milk, one cup flour, one teaspoon baking powder, one egg, one tablespoon butter. Pour over tart apples (sliced) and bake in hot oven.

SNOWFLAKES
Miss Nora Neal

Combine as in mixing cake half a cup of butter, a cup of sugar, half a cup of milk, two cups of flour, a level tablespoonful of baking powder, and the whites of four eggs. Turn into buttered cups and steam half an hour. Turn out, roll in powdered sugar and serve with any preferred fruit sauce

SNOW PUDDING
Ella McClure

One and a half cups water, one-half cup sugar, one-half salt spoon of salt, well mixed and brought to a boiling point. Wet three tablespoons of cornstarch in one-quarter cup cold water; stir into boiling syrup and cook ten minutes. Beat whites of three eggs to a dry froth and whip the boiling mixture into them. Return to fire one minute to set the egg, adding one-half cup lemon juice and a quarter of a grated rind. Turn into a mold that has been wet in cold water and set away to become ice cold. Serve with a soft custard made with yolks of eggs.

QUEEN OF PUDDINGS
Mrs. E. R. Beitzell, Des Moines, Iowa

One pint broken bits of bread, one cup sugar, yolks of three eggs, one quart milk (scant) one tablespoon butter melted and browned; bake, then spread layer of jelly on top and cover with beaten whites, brown a few moments in oven.

ROLLED APPLE DUMPLINGS
A. P. E O.

Make a rich baking powder biscuit dough; roll it out in a sheet less than half an inch thick. Cover thickly with chopped apples and roll up as compactly as possible. Cut this roll into sections nearly two inches thick, placing these in a dripping pan. Mix one dessert spoon of flour through one cup sugar, add generous cup of cold water and cook ten minutes. Pour this over the dumplings; grate a little nutmeg over them and bake a good brown. Serve with cream and sugar.

BAKED APPLE DUMPLINGS
Mrs. Cyrus Mentzer

Peel and core good baking apples and fill cavities with sugar. Make paste same as for baking powder biscuits as soft as can be handled and encase apples. Put dumplings in deep pan and almost cover with boiling water into which put lump of butter size of an egg and generous cup of sugar. Dust a little flour over for thickening. Bake 45 minutes or until they are light brown. Serve with cream or hot sauce.

HASTY PUDDING
Mrs. C. C. Cunningham

To six eggs beaten lightly add one quart sweet milk, six tablespoons flour and one saltspoon salt; beat all lightly, put in buttered pan and bake in very hot oven. Serve while hot with hard sauce.

HARD SAUCE

Butter size of egg, cream all the sifted powdered sugar into butter that it will take, and flavor with lemon or vanilla extract.

KLUM ROLL
Oskaloosa King's Daughters Cook Book

Add three teaspoons of baking powder and one teaspoon salt to one quart of flour, rub in two tablespoons butter, add enough sweet milk to make a soft dough; roll out; sprinkle with one cup chopped seeded raisins, dust with cinnamon, roll up and steam thirty minutes. Serve warm with sauce.

COLD SAUCE (For Puddings)
Maria Ball

Four tablespoonsful of butter, six tablespoonsful of sugar, the white of one egg, a wine-glassful of wine. Beat the butter and sugar until very white, beat the egg and add it; then the wine slowly, season with fresh lemon or orange.

RICH WINE SAUCE
Dickie Cornell Gebhardt

One cupful of butter, two of powdered sugar, one-half cup of wine. Beat butter to a cream; add sugar gradually and when light add the wine, which has been made hot, a little at a time. Place all in a double boiler and stir two minutes. Should then be smooth and foamy.

HARD SAUCE
Mrs. W. P. Gibson

Cream a cup of powdered sugar and a quarter of cup of butter; beat in juice of one lemon. When light and creamy add beaten whites of two eggs and whip all together. Grate a little nutmeg over top and set on ice to harden. Vanilla may be used with nutmeg if desired.

TAPIOCA PUDDING
Mrs. Della Myers

Soak one-half cup tapioca four hours, add one quart sweet milk, one cup sugar, one-half cup raisins, four eggs, save whites for meringue. Bake in moderate oven.

SAUCE FOR PLUM PUDDING
Maria Ball

One coffee cupful of sugar, one of butter; beat well together. Break an egg in and mix well. Put on the stove and stir until melted; add two tablespoons wine, pour up immediately.

PLUM PUDDING SAUCE
Mrs. Maude Mentzer

One cup sugar, one egg, piece of butter size of walnut, one tablespoon flour, two tablespoons cold water; beat up all together and pour into half pint of milk. Flavor with wine or vanilla.

FIG PUDDING
Mrs. Edith Ogle

One cup seeded raisins, one cup chopped figs, one cup chopped suet, one cup sweet milk, two and one-half cups flour, one cup Orleans molasses, one teaspoon soda, one teaspoon ginger, one teaspoon cinnamon, one teaspoon nutmeg. Mix suet well in flour like for pie crust. Steam three hours in cake pan; keep covered until done. Serve with sauce.

SUET PUDDING
Mrs. Adda Roberts

One cup finely chopped suet, one cup molasses, one cup sweet milk, one cup seeded raisins (floured), one-half cup currants, three cups flour (half graham and half wheat flour), one teaspoon baking powder sifted in flour. Steam three hours. Flour the pudding bag.

SAUCE

One and one-half cups sugar, one and one-half tablespoons flour. Moisten with three or four tablespoons of vinegar. Add one-fourth grated nutmeg and a pinch of salt. Pour over this one and one-half pints boiling water. Add a spoonful of butter and let it come to the boil again.

PASTRY

"The carrot red and the cabbage head,
With the squash and the onion vie;
But who can tell his emotions well,
At the thoughts of a pumpkin pie?"

PUMPKIN PIE
Anna M. Donley, Everist, Iowa

One cup pumpkin, one cup milk, two-thirds cup sugar, yolks of two eggs, one tablespoon flour, saltspoon salt, cinnamon, nutmeg and ginger to suit the taste. Put this mixture in your pan, beat the whites of the eggs stiff and stir in lightly.   Bake rather slowly.

PUMPKIN PIE
Mrs. S. D. McClelland

Peel the pumpkin, remove seeds and the stringy parts.   Cut in small pieces and steam.   When done beat to a cream with large spoon; press through sieve.   To each quart of pumpkin, add three well-beaten eggs, a heaping coffee cup sugar, one pint of new milk, one teaspoon each of ginger and nutmeg, half teaspoon allspice and tablespoon melted butter.   Line pans with crust. Bake half done, remove from oven and fill with pumpkin and bake again until a light brown.

CHOCOLATE PIE
Mrs. Will C. Reed, Pleasantville. Iowa

One-half cup sugar, three teaspoons flour, two tablespoons chocolate, yolks of two eggs.   Milk sufficient to fill pan, beat two whites for top.

CREAM PIE
Mrs. J. Risser

Cover a pie pan with puff paste and spread with one tablespoon butter, mix two tablespoons flour with one cup sugar and put on butter, then a cup of cream and some grated nutmeg.   Do not stir ingredients together.

East Ward School House

CHOCOLATE PIE

Mrs. A. B. Culver

Line a deep pan with rich pie crust and bake in a quick oven. Grate one-half teacup chocolate and put into a sauce pan with one cup of hot water, butter size of an egg, one cup of sugar, the beaten yolks of two eggs and two tablespoons of cornstarch dissolved in a little water. Mix well; cook until thick, stirring constantly. Pour into pie shell and let cool. Beat the whites of the two eggs to a stiff froth, add two tablespoons sugar, spread on top of pie and slightly brown in oven.

CREAM PIE

Nan Cornell

One pint of milk—half of which boil—the other half to mix the filling. One tablespoon of butter, two-thirds cup of sugar, three tablespoons of flour. Mix flour and sugar together, last yolks of two eggs and remaining milk. Return to fire and cook until thick, stirring constantly. Flavor with vanilla. Bake crust, add filling. Beat whites of eggs for top. Put in oven to brown.

RICE LEMON PIE

Oskaloosa King's Daughters' Cook Book

Boil till done one teacup rice, sweeten, and flavor with vanilla; line a baking pan with it; turn into it a lemon custard made as follows: Yolks of two eggs, teacup of sugar, half cup butter, two cups new milk, juice of two lemons, grated rind of one, one tablespoon cornstarch; this should be cooked till thick before putting into rice pastry. Set in oven to brown, then make a meringue of the whites of the two eggs and four tablespoons powdered sugar flavored with lemon. Place in a moderate oven and let it brown slowly.

BOSTON CREAM PIE
Burnie Woodruff

Crust—Two eggs beaten separately, one-half cup sugar, two-thirds cup of flour, two tablespoons of milk or water, one teaspoon baking powder. Cream—One cup milk boiled, one-half cup sugar, one-fourth cup flour, one egg, butter size of an egg.

LEMON PIE
Della Myers

Juice of one lemon, one and one-half cups sugar, one and one-half pints water, three tablespoons cornstarch, three eggs; save whites for meringue. This makes enough for two pies.

LEMON PIE
Mrs. Nellie Clark, Carroll, Iowa

Juice and grated rind of one lemon, yolks of two eggs, one cup boiling water, one tablespoon cornstarch mixed with a little cold water, add one cup sugar, lump of butter size of a walnut. Cook until clear. Add juice and eggs to this. Meringue on top. Bake shell first.

LEMON PIE
Mrs. A. D. Steele

Grate one lemon, add one cup of sugar, five eggs, (save whites of two eggs), one cup cold water, one tablespoon of flour. Mix thoroughly and bake with undercrust only. When pie is done, spread over top whites of the two eggs beaten stiff with one tablespoon of sugar. Return pie to oven until it is golden brown.

ORANGE PIE
Mrs. Frank Dunlap

Grate rind and add juice of one orange, one-half cup sugar, one tablespoon flour or cornstarch, yolks of two eggs, white of one, one tablespoon melted butter, milk to fill pie dish. White of one egg beaten and placed on top when pie is baked. Brown in oven.

CRANBERRY PIE
Mrs. Adah Gaiser

Two and one-half cups sugar, one cup boiling water, one-half cup cornstarch, one-half cup maple syrup, one tablespoon butter, one quart cranberries. Add sugar, two and one-half cups (above mentioned), to the boiling water, dissolve cornstarch in cold water and add to the sugar and water, then add the syrup, stir until thick, then add berries, butter and pinch of salt. Cook until done. Serve in one crust with whipped cream.

RAISIN PIE
Mrs. J. A. J. Powers

One cup of raisins ground fine, mix with two well-beaten eggs, one cup of milk, one-half cup of sugar, butter size of an egg and one spoonful of flour. Mix well together and boil until thick. Fill single crust and bake. Put beaten whites of eggs on top, if so desired.

SQUASH PIE
Mrs. Walter Jenkins

Boil the squash until well done, add a little salt and press through a coarse sieve, then to every teacupful of squash add one cupful of milk, one-half cup sugar, one egg, one teaspoonful flour, nutmeg and cinnamon to taste. (A pinch of soda, sweet cream or a small piece of butter adds to the flavor of the pie.) Line a pie plate with paste and fill.

CUSTARD PIE
Mrs. Lizzie H. Underhill

One quart milk (new preferred), four eggs, one scant teacup granulated sugar. If the eggs are large, add one-half teacup of milk. To prevent soggy crust have the oven very hot when pie is first put in, or until the paste begins to puff.

ENGLISH WALNUT PIE
Mrs. Chas. Fagan, Ft. Madison, Iowa

Beat the yolks of two eggs and one-half cup sugar to a cream, add a tablespoon of lemon juice, the juice and half the grated rind of an orange and one-half cup of English walnuts. Line a deep pie pan with pastry and when half baked add the filling and finish baking. Cover with frosting made of the whites of two eggs, two tablespoons sugar and two tablespoons chopped walnut meats.

COCOANUT PIE
Mrs. Fannie M. Chamberlain

Whites of eight eggs, one cup cocoanut, three-fourths cup sugar, one quart milk, small pinch salt, butter size of walnut, four tablespoons of flour. Put sugar, cocoanut, salt and butter into milk and steam until boiling. Mix flour with enough cold milk to make a thin batter; pour this into boiling milk. Beat whites of four of the eggs and stir lightly into the milk. Flavor with vanilla. Bake crust before putting in filling. Beat whites of remaining four eggs with a little sugar and spread over pie. Put into oven and brown. This amount of filling makes two pies. Exceedingly rich and delicious.

COCOANUT TARTS
Mrs. Will C. Reed, Pleasantville, Iowa

Yolks of four eggs, one cup sugar, one-fourth cup water, butter size of egg, and one-half box of cocoanut; bake in crusts in a moderate oven.

PEACH DOLLY
Flora Pitsor

Three-fourths pound of evaporated peaches soaked over night; pour off water, put on fresh. Cook until tender. When almost done sweeten to taste. Make short cake, mash peaches, spread between layers. Serve with cream.

PEACH COBBLER
Mrs. Alice Bellamy

One quart of peaches, one egg, one cup of milk, two tablespoons butter melted, one cup of flour, one teaspoon baking powder. Turn the peaches into a pudding pan. Make a batter of the remaining ingredients, pour over the peaches and bake. Serve with cream.

RHUBARB PIE
Mrs. Georgia Black, in Congregational Cook Book

Three and one-half cups rhubarb, two cups sugar, two cups seeded raisins and two eggs. This is sufficient for three pies.

SWEET POTATO PIE
Mrs. Elsie Worstell

One-half pint mashed sweet potatoes, one cup sugar, two and one-half cups milk, one teaspoon ginger, one teaspoon cinnamon, pinch of salt, four eggs, saving out whites of two for meringue. This makes three pies.

STRAWBERRY PIE
Florence Gamble

Into a rich, deep under crust that has been baked, put strawberries enough to fill, and cover with sugar, lightly. Make a meringue of the whites of two eggs and four tablespoons of sugar, cover the pie with it and brown. (Fine.)

STRAWBERRY SHORT CAKE
Adda Roberts

Beat together one egg, one-half cup sugar, lump of butter the size of an egg, two cups sweet milk, two teaspoonfuls of baking powder and flour enough to make a batter as for cake. Bake in layers for 20 minutes. Split and add berries, sugar and cream.

STRAWBERRY SHORT CAKE
Emily S. Cooper

Sift together one quart flour, two teaspoons baking powder, one teaspoon salt. Mix with this one tablespoon each of lard and butter, and enough milk to make a very soft dough. Cut into biscuits and bake two together with butter between. Mash two quarts strawberries, sweeten, and as soon as the biscuits are taken from the oven, separate, butter, fill with berries, place some on top; serve on individual plates with cream.

STRAWBERRY SHORT CAKE
Mrs. Marie Vawter

Take two cups sifted flour and two teaspoons baking powder, sift and mix through flour, mix two tablespoons heaping full of cold butter through the flour and mix into a soft dough with sweet milk. Roll out and cover a large pie plate, spread with butter and roll another thickness and put on; bake in a quick oven. Take off upper crust and butter well the inside of both layers. If strawberries are gritty, wash carefully and sprinkle with plenty of sugar and let them stand half an hour to drain the juice out before the short cake is baked. Fill immediately and serve hot or cold.

MINCE MEAT
Mrs. Nora Elliott

Five pounds of lean beef, three pounds of sugar, two pounds of butter, two pounds of raisins, two pounds of currants, one pound of citron, one pound of figs, one pound of blanched almonds, two pounds suet chopped fine, one peck of tart apples, one pint of vinegar, one pint of molasses, one pint of good brandy, one nutmeg, one tablespoon cloves, four of cinnamon, two of allpice, one of black pepper; add enough boiled cider to make moist.

MINCE MEAT

Stella Woodruff Wright

Four pounds meat, two pounds suet, eight pounds apples, four pounds sugar, two pounds raisins, three tablespoons cinnamon, one nutmeg, one quart boiled cider and fruit juices to suit the taste or two quarts cider alone, one-half pint molasses or sugar, one-half teacup salt, two-thirds package of candied citron, lemon and orange mixed.

PASTRY FOR UNDER CRUST

Mrs. Marie Vawter

Three large tablespoons of flour, rubbing into it a large tablespoon of lard with a pinch of salt, mixing with ice water enough to make a smooth, stiff paste.

PIE CRUST FOR ONE PIE

Mrs. C. E. Hon

One cup flour, two tablespoons lard, three table-spoons cold water, pinch salt and baking powder. Mix quickly.

HINTS ON PIE CRUST

Contributed by P. E. O.'s

No. 1. When you have pies ready for the oven, to pour cold water over the crust and drain off will make them crisp and a beautiful brown.

No. 2. When you make a pie, let the upper crust extend about an inch over the plate. When all the pie is finished, with floured fingers carefully lift the under crust and tuck the left-over piece under the bottom. Pinch all around and it cannot leak, no matter how juicy.

PUFF PASTE

Mrs G. W Baxter, Telford, Tenn.

One pound best butter, one pound pastry flour, one scant teaspoon salt, about one cup ice water. (By measure one quart flour and one pint butter.) Wash butter in cold water, divide in four parts, pat until thin, wrap in napkin and place on ice. Mix salt with flour, rub in one part butter, add ice water slowly, mix with knife and cut till it can be taken up clear from bowl, toss out on well-floured board; pat into flat cake, roll out until one-half inch thick. Roll one part of butter thin and lay on middle of paste, fold sides toward middle, then ends over and double again; pat and roll out again; repeat this process with remaining pieces of butter, and when butter is all rubbed in, the paste should be rolled and folded till no streaks of butter can be seen. After last rolling place on ice to harden, as it may then be cut and shaped more easily.

Jelly Roll   Cora

4 eggs   1 cup sugar
2 tablespoonsful milk   1 cup flour
½ teaspon B. P.

---

1 lb fat pork ground - fine, pour over
this 1 pt boiling water, 2 cups sugar
1 cup mollasses 2 taspons cinnamon
1 taspon cloves + nutmeg 1 soda
1 or two lbs. raisens or currents
6 cups flour.

Main Street Looking West from Marion County National Bank

Chilli Sauce

24 tomatoes

6   green peppers

5 cts   cinnamon

4 large or 6 small onions

2   stalks celery

8 table spoons B. sugar

6   cups vinegar

2 table-spoons salt.

Cinnamon Cake.

2 cups brown sugar

½ cup lard

2 eggs.

1 cup sour milk

1 teaspoon soda.

spices to suit taste

2 cups flour.

Branbury Cakes.

2 lemons grated rind and juice 2 cups of
raisens ground. 1/2 cup sugar two eggs well
beaten, crust like pie.

Burnt Sugar Cake.

1 1/2 cups sugar, 1/2 cup butter,
2 eggs beaten, 1 cup water
2 teaspoonful B. P., 2 1/2 cups flour.
1 teaspoon vanilla, 3 teaspoonful burnt sugar.

Date Cake.

1 1/2 cups sugar   1/2 cup butter
1 egg   4 teaspoon B. P.
3 cups flour   1 cup milk
1 cup dates cut fbured, bake in loaf.

Angle Food   Grandma Nass.

11 egg whites beaten stiff.
1 1/2 tumbler sugar
1 tumbler flour
1 teaspoon cream of tartar a little lemon extract.

COOKIES, DOUGHNUTS. TEA CAKES, GINGERBREAD

"With weights and measures just and true,
Oven of even heat;
Well-buttered tins and quiet nerves,
Success will be complete."

OATMEAL COOKIES
Maude Wright

Two eggs, one cup sugar, one cup butter and lard, seven tablespoons sour milk, one teaspoon soda, one cup raisins, two cups oatmeal, two cups flour, pinch of salt, one tablespoon of cinnamon.

OAT MEAL COOKIES
Mrs. R. C. Nace

Two eggs, one cup sugar (dark), one cup shortening, two cups oatmeal, two cups flour, three tablespoons sour milk, one level teaspoon soda, salt. Flavor with vanilla, mix well and drop with teaspoon on floured bread pan, allowing plenty of room to spread.

RAISIN COOKIES
Alice Culver

One and a half cups sugar, one cup butter, three eggs well beaten, one cup chopped raisins, one teaspoon soda dissolved in a little sour milk, one teaspoon cinnamon and nutmeg mixed. Roll a little thicker than ordinary cookies.

NUT COOKIES
Mrs. G. E. McCorkle

Two eggs, one cup of butter, one cup of sugar, one-half teaspoon of soda, one cup of chopped nuts. Use just enough flour so they can be rolled thin.

FRUIT COOKIES
Mrs. Walter Elliott

One cup of milk, one and a half cups of sugar, three and a half cups of flour, one cup of nuts, one-half cup of currants, one-half cup of raisins, one cup of butter, three eggs, one teaspoon soda dissolved in one and a half teaspoons of water, one-half teaspoon of salt, one teaspoon of cinnamon.

WALNUT COOKIES
Mrs. Charles Fagan, Ft. Madison, Iowa

One cup butter, one and one-half cups sugar, three eggs, two cups chopped walnuts, one and a half cups of flour, one cup flour mixed with nuts, one teaspoon baking powder. Cream butter and sugar together, add eggs, then the flour mixed with nuts. Sift baking powder and the one and a half cups of flour together and add the last thing. Drop by spoonfuls on buttered tins, allowing ample room for spreading. Before baking decorate top of each cake with half a nut and dust with gratulated sugar. Bake in moderate oven.

CREAM COOKIES
Mrs. M. C Bellamy

One egg, one cup sugar, one cup of sour cream, one teaspoon of soda, one-half teaspoon grated nutmeg, flour enough to handle. Roll thin, sprinkle with sugar and bake in hot oven.

AMMONIA COOKIES
Nora White

Three eggs, two cups sugar, one cup sweet milk, one and a half cups butter, two tablespoons baking ammonia powdered and dissolved in milk. Mix rather stiff, roll very thin and bake in hot oven. (Are improved with age.)

SUGAR COOKIES

Mrs. L. K. Butterfield

Four eggs, one and two-thirds cups lard, two cups sugar, one cup milk, flavor to suit. Add flour to roll, three teaspoons baking powder, but do not mix whole amount stiff at first. Take a handful of dough and add flour enough to stiffen, then bake it before taking more. This prevents handling the dough too much, which often spoils cookies. Sour milk may be used with a teaspoon of soda.

SANTA CLAUS COOKIES

Mrs H. L Bousquet

Mix well six cups flour, three cups brown sugar, two and one-half cups butter, one-half teaspoon cloves, one teaspoon allspice, three teaspoons cinnamon, then add one-half cup of water (no more), one scant teaspoon soda. Bake in moderate oven until brown.

HOT WATER GINGER BREAD

Tone Bros., Des Moines, Iowa

(This is the famous $150.00 Gingerbread Recipe)

One cup New Orleans molasses, one-half cup brown sugar, two tablespoons butter, melted, one-half cup boiling water, one egg lightly beaten, two cups pastry flour or one and three-fourths cups bread flour, one level teaspoon (scant) soda, one-half teaspoon salt, one teaspoon Tone's Jamaica Ginger. Sift dry ingredients all together. Pour molasses into mixing bowl and stir in sugar and melted butter, add dry ingredients and hot water, lastly egg beaten very lightly. Bake in dripping pan in moderate oven thirty minutes. Serve hot with fresh, unsalted butter. This is excellent.

GINGER BREAD
Prue Collins

One cup butter, one and three-fourth cups sugar, one cup sour cream, one tablespoon ginger, one good teaspoon soda, one teaspoon cinnamon, one cup raisins, two and one-half cups flour. Add two unbeaten eggs last thing and stir hard.

GINGER BREAD
Mrs. Ota Rietveld, Pella, Iowa

First: One cup sour milk, one cup sugar, one cup molasses. Second: Two-thirds cup melted butter, three cups flour, two teaspoons ginger, one-half teaspoon cloves, one-half teaspoon cinnamon, one-half teaspoon soda. Put together the first; mix well, then add the rest. Then add two unbeaten eggs, put in pans thin.

PEANUT COOKIES
Mrs. W. R. Myers

One-third cup butter, one-half cup sugar, two eggs, one and one-half cups flour, one-half teaspoon salt, one cup finely chopped peanuts, one and one-half teaspoons baking powder, one-third cup milk, one teaspoon lemon juice. Drop by spoonfuls on greased pans, bake about ten minutes in a quick oven.

GINGER COOKIES
Estella W. Wright

Two cups molasses, one cup sweet milk, one-half cup butter, one-half cup lard, two teaspoons soda, one teaspoon ginger. Stir stiff with flour and bake into cookies next morning. This mixture may be kept in a crock in a cool place, rolling out a batch of fresh cookies at any time—the last are the best.

GINGER COOKIES
Mrs. M. C. Bellamy

One cup sugar, one cup butter and lard mixed, one tablespoon of cinnamon, one cup sorghum molasses, one tablespoon of ginger, one tablespoon soda, dissolved in one half cup cold water, flour to roll good.

GINGER SNAPS
Mrs. G. K. Hart

Two cups molasses, one cup of sugar, one cup of lard or butter, one-half cup boiling water on soda, one dessert spoon of soda, one of ginger, one of cinnamon, flour.

GINGER BALLS
Lucy Huber, Pella, Iowa

One cup sugar, one cup molasses, two-thirds cup lard, two eggs, one tablespoon ginger, three cups flour, half teaspoon salt, one tablespoon soda, one cup boiling water. Mix sugar, lard, salt, molasses and ginger, then the eggs, well beaten, add flour and mix well. Pour the boiling water over the soda and add to the batter. Drop with a spoon in hot greased tins.

ROCKS
Mrs. E. W. Coxe, Red Oak, Iowa

One cup butter, one and a half cups granulated sugar, three and a half cups flour, three eggs, one teaspoon soda in half cup of coffee, one cup of nuts, or two if you want, two packages raisins cut in two or three pieces, one tablespoon cinnamon, half teaspoon cloves, half teaspoon allspice, one nutmeg. Mix your butter and sugar, then add the beaten eggs and coffee with the soda dissolved in it, then the flour a little at a time, so you get it well mixed, then the fruit and nuts. It must be so stiff you can hardly stir it. Have your pans hot; do not wash between times, rub with buttered cloth.

HERMITS
Clara Hastings, Roswell, N. M.

Two cups brown sugar, half cup sour milk, one cup butter, half teaspoon soda, one cup chopped raisins, half teaspoon cinnamon, three eggs, half nutmeg, flour to make stiff dough. Roll and cut with biscuit cutter and bake in moderate oven.

DELICIOUS DOUGHNUTS
Mrs. W. M. Black

Soak one cake of yeast in lukewarm water at noon, add flour to make thick batter. Keep in warm place till evening. Then take one pint of warm milk, one-half cup butter, one of sugar, one-half teaspoonful salt, yolks of three eggs beaten light, add enough flour to make a stiff dough. Put in warm place and let rise over night. Beat well in the morning, let rise again then roll out on kneading board half an inch thick, cut in small squares, drop one-half teaspoonful of strawberry or raspberry jam on squares, fold over, pressing edges firmly together, let rise until light; fry in hot lard and sprinkle with powered sugar. These are fine with coffee.

DOUGHNUTS
Mrs. Josie Boydston

Two cups sugar, butter size of walnut, four well-beaten eggs, one cup milk, five teaspoons of baking powder, flour enough to make stiff dough; roll out small piece of dough at a time. Cut and have lard hot.

DOUGHNUTS
Mrs. L. M. Cox, Pella, Iowa.

One cup granulated sugar, one cup sweet milk, four tablespoons melted butter, two eggs, three cups unsifted flour sifted with three tablespoons baking powder, one-half teaspoon salt, one teaspoon vanilla, sufficient flour to roll out. Sugar while warm.

Congregational Church

DOUGHNUTS
Mrs. G. K. Hart

One and one-half cups of sugar, three cups of flour, piece of butter size of an egg, three eggs, one cup of milk, one teaspoonful of mace or nutmeg, two of baking powder.

[handwritten annotations: "cups 1/3 reigen", "2 cups", "" 2 eggs", "2/3 milk", "nutmeg", "teaspoon, 1 1/3 to pint"]

CRULLERS
Luta Parsons

One and one-half cupsful of sugar, one cupful of sour milk, two eggs, two scant tablespoonsful of melted butter, half a nutmeg, grated, one large teaspoonful of cinnamon, one teaspoonful of salt, one teaspoonful of soda, enough flour to make a little stiffer than biscuit dough. Roll out a quarter of an inch thick and cut with a fried-cake cutter with a hole in the center. Fry in hot lard.

GINGER BREAD
Mrs. Lillie Young

One pint molasses, one cup butter or lard, one cup water, one cup sugar, one tablespoon soda in hot water, one tablespoon ginger, one teaspoon cinnamon, flour.

TEA CAKES
Mrs. Gertie McClymond

Two and one-half cups pastry flour, one heaping teaspoon baking powder, one and one-half cups sugar, one-half teaspoon salt, one egg, one cup milk, one tablespoon melted butter. Mix in order given and bake in gem pans.

FIG DROP CAKES
Alice Culver

One cup sugar, one-half cup butter, one-fourth cup milk, two cups flour, three-fourths teaspoon baking powder, one cup chopped figs; drop by teaspoonsful on baking sheet or pan and bake in moderately quick oven for eight minutes.

DEVIL'S FOOD GEMS
Isabel C. Hays

One cup of brown or white sugar, two tablespoons or scant half cup of butter beaten to a cream; add beaten yolks of two eggs, and one-third cup of grated chocolate melted in a little warm water; also one teaspoon soda dissolved in same; then add one teaspoon of vanilla, two-thirds cup of milk, two cups of flour in which is sifted one teaspoon of baking powder; last add the stiffly beaten whites of two eggs; bake in gem pans.

CORN STARCH PUFFS
Mrs. John Reed

One cup cornstarch, one cup pulverized sugar, one-half cup butter, two teaspoons baking powder, one teaspoon vanilla, cream butter and sugar together, then add the yolks of four eggs, beat the whites very stiff and add alternately with cornstarch; bake in gem pans which should be well greased and heated before putting the mixture in.

CREAM PUFFS
Cora Wolf

One cup butter in one cup hot water, stir one cup of flour in this, let it stay on stove long enough to cook, stirring all the time; when cool stir in three eggs, if eggs are large two will do. Filling: Whip one egg to a foam, and put in one cup of milk, two tablespoons sugar; cook until thick, stirring all the time. When puffs are baked and cold put in the filling.

VANITIES
Mrs. Wm. Jenkins

Four eggs, one tablespoon water, one-half teaspoon salt, two tablespoons sugar, one-half teaspoon of baking powder, enough flour to make a very stiff dough; roll as thin as paper, cut in squares and drop in hot lard. They burn quickly. When cool powder with pulverized sugar.

OATMEAL MACAROONS
Mrs. Mell Woodruff

One large tablespoon butter (melted), one cup of granulated sugar, two cups rolled oats, two eggs well beaten, two teaspoons of baking powder, one teaspoon vanilla; add flour enough to make stiff; pat about single teaspoonful into tiny cake, drop on greased pan about two inches apart with blanched almond on top of each. Bake quickly.

HICKORYNUT JUMBLES
Emily Collins, Bay City, Mich.

Grate one large cup of nuts, rub one cup of butter with one and a half cups of sugar; add three beaten eggs, whites and yolks separately, two tablespoons of milk and five cups of sifted flour; then add by degrees the grated nuts, so as to make a stiff dough; roll them and cut with small cutter; bake in quick oven five to ten minutes.

NUT CAKES
Mary E. Steele

Beat four eggs until very light, add one pint of sugar, beat thoroughly; fold in one pint of flour and one pint of hickory nut meats, chopped fine. Drop batter by teaspoonfuls on greased pans and bake in hot oven. This quantity makes three dozen cakes.

AUNTY'S MOLASSES CAKE
Mrs. C. C. Cunningham

Two teacups molasses (Orleans is best) one-half cup butter (or melted lard), two eggs, one teacup sour milk, two teaspoons soda, a pinch of salt if lard is used; flavor with nutmeg; use flour enough to make thin batter and bake in slow oven.

CAKES
LOAF, LAYER, ICINGS, FILLINGS

"I wish my wife no cake would make,
Or else some cooking lessons take."

LOAF

SPICE CAKE
Mrs. Ella Everett

Two cups sugar, one cup butter, half cup sweet milk, one cup mashed potatoes, half cup chocolate, two cups flour, four eggs, two teaspoons baking powder, one teaspoon cloves, one teaspoon cinnamon, one teaspoon allspice, one teaspoon nutmeg, one teaspoon vanilla, one teaspoon lemon, one cup chopped nuts.

SPICE CAKE
Mrs. H. M. Dickerson

One and a half cups sugar, two eggs, one cup sour milk, one cup raisins, one tablespoon butter, one level teaspoon soda, one teaspoon cinnamon, three teaspoons grated chocolate, two cups flour. Sift chocolate and cinnamon with flour. Bake in large dripping pan.

FRUIT CAKE
Mrs. J. B. Elliott

Two cups butter, three cups light brown sugar, one cup New Orleans molasses, two cups sour milk, four eggs, five cups flour, one cup chopped almonds, two pounds raisins, one pound currants, one pound citron, one pound figs, one-half pint brandy, two teaspoons soda; spice and nutmeg to taste.

The Hanks Store

FRUIT CAKE
Maude Wright

One large cup sugar, two-thirds cup butter, two eggs, one small cup sour cream or milk, one teaspoon soda, one cup of raisins, one cup of nuts, chopped, three small cups of flour, one tablespoon cinnamon. Bake slowly one hour.

COMMON FRUIT CAKE
Estella Wright

One cup sugar (large), two-thirds cup butter, one cup sour cream (small), if very rich use scant one-half cup butter, one teaspoon of soda, two eggs, one-fourth teaspoon cinnamon, one-fourth teaspoon cloves, one teacup raisins, one-fourth cup hickory nuts, two small cups flour; spread with caramel icing. One cup brown sugar, two tablespoons cream, (add a teaspoon of butter if poor cream), one-half teaspoon vanilla; boil two minutes, remove and beat to a cream; add one-half teaspoon vanilla.

FRUIT CAKE
Mrs. J. V. Brann

One pound sugar, three-fourths pound of butter creamed light, one wine glass brandy, one dozen ground cloves, one teaspoon ground cinnamon, one-fourth pound citron, ten eggs beaten separately—use yolks first, two pounds cleaned currants rubbed in flour, one pound raisins cut fine, one pound seeded and left whole, one pound sifted flour; stir in citron, currants and chopped raisins and lastly whole raisins with flour alternately; then whites of eggs beaten stiff. Bake in moderate oven; decrease heat last hour; bake two hours, line pan with buttered paper and put a piece on top; will keep several months; should be a few weeks old before using.

DEVIL'S FOOD
Lucy Huber, Pella, Iowa

Dissolve two ounces sweet chocolate in five table-spoons of boiling water, cream ha. ;up butter with one and a half cups sugar, add yolks of four eggs well beaten, then the chocolate, half cup sweet milk, one and three-fourth cups flour, two tablespoons baking powder, one teaspoon vanilla, add whites of eggs last.

DEVIL'S CAKE
Mrs. E. W. Coxe, Red Oak, Iowa

One and a half cups sugar, one and a half cups but-ter, three eggs, two teaspoons vanilla, one small teaspoon soda in half cup warm water, three-fourths cup Baker's chocolate, grated; pour half cup boiling water over choc-olate and thoroughly dissolve. Two and one-fourth cups flour sifted. Stir all together and prepare for oven as quickly as possible. Bake forty-five minutes.

CHOCOLATE CAKE
Millie W. Baker, Chicago

One and a half cups sugar, two-thirds cup butter, one cup milk, three eggs, two cups flour, one square of chocolate, one small teaspoon vanilla, two heaping tea-spoons baking powder. Bake in moderate oven, not opening oven door, for twenty minutes.

BLACK CAKE
Mrs. F. P. Grant

One-fourth cake chocolate, grated; one teaspoon soda stirred into chocolate. Pour one-half cup boiling water over them. Two cups C sugar, one-half cup but-ter, three eggs, two and a half cups flour, one-half cup sour milk.

COFFEE CAKE

Mrs. E. L. Syp

Two cups sugar, one cup molasses, one cup butter, one cup cold coffee, fo cups flour, four eggs, one cup of raisins, one teaspoon soda, one of cinnamon, one of cloves, one of nutmeg.

COFFEE CAKE

Mrs. O. J. Kendig

Three cups of sugar, one cup of butter, one cup of cold coffee, four cups of flour, three teaspoons of baking powder, four eggs beaten separately, one teaspoon of cloves and one tablespoon of cinnamon, one nutmeg, one pound of raisins, one-half pound of currants, citron if desired.

NUT CAKE

Mrs. G. K. Hart

Two scant cups of sugar, one cup of milk, two-thirds cup of butter, four eggs, three cups of flour, one and one-half teaspoons of baking powder, one cup of walnuts chopped. Mix together and add the nuts and white of eggs last.

NUT CAKE

Mrs. Cook, Pella, Iowa

Cream one-half cup butter and one cup sugar and beat light, add the yolks of two eggs well beaten, one-half cup milk alternately with one and one-half cups of flour sifted with three level teaspoons of baking powder, then one cup of chopped nut meats and the whites of two eggs. Bake in a sheet. Ice with chocolate frosting and mark in squares with a half of an English walnut meat in each square.

NUT CAKE
Mary E. Steele

One cup of butter and two cups of sugar beaten to a cream, five eggs (or whites of eight eggs, if preferred), one cup of cold water, three and one-half cups of flour, two teaspoons baking powder, one teaspoon lemon and vanilla mixed, one cup of hickory nut meats chopped very fine.

WHITE CITRON CAKE
Luta Parsons

Cream one cup of butter with two cups of sugar, add one cup of milk, three cups of flour sifted with three level teaspoons of baking powder and last the whites of five eggs beaten stiff. Stir in one cup of finely shaved citron the last thing and bake in two loaves or in one large loaf.

WHITE LOAF CAKE
Mrs. Mell Woodruff

One cup butter, two cups sugar (granulated), one cup sweet milk, whites of eight eggs, three cups angel food flour, one tablespoon cornstarch, two rounding teaspoons baking powder, one teaspoon vanilla. Use same size cup in measuring all ingredients. First measure butter and cream with one cup sifted sugar, then add other cup sugar, beat well, measure flour, add baking powder and cornstarch and sift five times. Put about one-third of milk in creamed butter and sugar, mix well, then add one-third flour and so continue until milk and flour are all used. Beat well between additions to ingredients. Last add beaten whites of eggs. If eggs are large seven will be sufficient. Do not stir dough after adding the eggs only sufficient to fold in the dough.

Main Buildings State Inebriate Hospital

POTATO CAKE
Mrs. Kate Crawford.

One cup butter, two cups flour, two cups sugar, four eggs, one-half cup milk, one cup raisins, one cup grated chocolate, one cup currants, one cup chopped nuts, one cup mashed potatoes, one teaspoon cinnamon, cloves, allspice, lemon and vanilla, two heaping teaspoons baking powder; cream butter and sugar, add milk, eggs beaten stiff, and other ingredients; flour the raisins and currants; add flour last; bake in loaf or layers, put together with white icing.

SUNSHINE CAKE
Lncy Bellamy

Whites of seven eggs, yolks of five eggs, one cup of flo??r, one cup of sugar, teaspoon cream tartar, flavoring. Sift the flour nine times, beat yolks of eggs and set aside; beat the whites stiff, then add cream of tartar; beat until very stiff. Beat the sugar into the whites of eggs; flavor and add flour.

MY MOTHER'S SPONGE CAKE
Belle Pollock

Three eggs well beaten, one cup sugar; beat these together, add two tablespoons water, one teaspoon baking powder, one cup flour.

MINNEHAHA CAKE
Mrs. M. D. Woodruff

One and one-half cups of white sugar, one-half cup butter, three eggs, two cups flour, two teaspoons baking powder, one cup sweet milk. For filling: Cook in about one-half cup of water, one pound of figs chopped fine, the juice of one-half lemon, and one-fourth cup of sugar.

SPONGE CAKE
Mrs. W. P. Gibson

Two eggs, one cup milk, one cup flour, two teaspoons baking powder, one-half cup boiling milk added last.

ANGEL FOOD
Mrs. F. M. Frush

Whites of thirteen small or twelve large eggs, one and one-half cups granulated sugar, one cup flour, one level teaspoon fresh cream tartar, one teaspoon vanilla. To the whites of eggs add a pinch of salt, then beat them stiff; add the sugar, which has been well sifted, then add the flour into which the cream tartar has been sifted. Last of all, the flavoring. After the eggs have been beaten to a stiff froth remove beater and use spoon to stir in the sugar and flour. Bake in Van Dorsen pan. Oven very slow at first. After the cake has risen to its height turn on the drafts and brown well. Remove from the oven and turn upside down to cool. Loosen sides and bottom and let the cake drop out.

CHOCOLATE MARBLE CAKE
Eva Belville

One-half cup butter, one cup sugar (fine granulated) beaten to a cream, add three-fourths cup of milk, two cups flour and two teaspoons baking powder. Beat these ingredients until mixed, then divide into two parts. To one part add, to make a dark portion, the yolks of four eggs, three tablespoons grated chocolate or cocoa, one tablespoon ground cinnamon, one teaspoon ground cloves, one teaspoon vanilla extract. To the white part add the whites of eggs (three whites will be sufficient, leaving one for icing) and one teaspoon lemon extract. Put in pan in alternate spoonsful light and dark and vice versa. Bake in a loaf and ice with either white or chocolate icing.

PRINCE OF WALES CAKE
Mrs. Nora Elliott

First part: One cup of light brown sugar, one-half cup butter, one-hàlf cup sour milk, two cups flour, one cup of raisins, yolks of three eggs, one teaspoon soda, one nutmeg. Second part—White part: one cup of granulated sugar, one cup of cornstarch, one-half cup butter, one cup flour, one-half cup sweet milk, two teaspoons of baking powder, whites of three eggs; flavor.

LOAF FIG CAKE
Dickie Cornell Gebhardt

One cup butter, one and one-half cups sugar beaten to a cream. Add one cup sweet milk and two and a half cups flour containing three teaspoons baking powder well sifted. Lastly add whites of eight eggs, well beaten or four whole eggs. Before mixing cake, prepare two pounds of figs by cutting (do not chop) into tiny bits and rubbing thoroughly with flour. Stir these into cake dough and immediately place in oven, baking from one and one-half to two hours. Will keep moist and nice for days.

MARBLE CAKE
Mrs. L. K. Butterfield

White part: One cup butter, two cups sugar, one cup sweet milk, three and one-half cups flour, one teaspoon baking powder, whites of eight eggs. Dark part: One cup butter, one cup sugar, one cup Orleans molasses, yolks of eight eggs, one cup sweet milk, four cups flour, two teaspoons baking powder, one teaspoon each nutmeg, cloves, cinnamon and vanilla. A small quantity of melted chocolate may be added. Drop dough in pan alternately or bake in sheets and cut in cubes.

RAISIN CAKE
Mrs. H. A. Shirer

Two eggs, one cup and half of light brown sugar, one-half cup butter, one cup chopped raisins, one cup sour milk, one teaspoon soda, flour enough to make quite stiff, one-half nutmeg, one teaspoon cloves; flavor.

FRUIT CAKE   (Without Wine)
Nora White

Mix one pound seedless raisins, one pound currants and one pound shredded citron. Flour them with one-half cup flour. Beat ten eggs without separating, very light. Cream one pound butter, add one pound sugar, and when very light, add the eggs and one pound flour. Beat well and add one teaspoon cinnamon, one teaspoon allspice, one-half teaspoon cloves, one nutmeg, grated rind and juice of one lemon and one orange. Beat and then stir in the fruit. Line pans with oiled paper. Steam for three hours and bake one.

LAYER

CHOCOLATE CAKE
Mrs. C. A. Reaver, Eldora, Iowa

Dissolve two squares of chocolate in five tablespoons of boiling water, cream one-half cup butter, adding gradually one and one-half cups sugar; add the yolks of four eggs beaten thoroughly, then add the chocolate, one-half cup milk, one and three-fourth cups flour, two rounding teaspoons baking powder, one teaspoon vanilla; beat the whites of eggs to a stiff froth and fold in the mixture carefully; bake in loaf or layer.

CHOCOLATE CAKE
Mrs. Chester Irvin

One and one-half cups sugar, one-half cup butter, beat to a cream, add the yolks of four eggs, well-beaten, one-half cup of warm water in which one-third cake of chocolate has been dissolved, two cups of flour in which one teaspoon of soda has been sifted, one-half cup full of sour milk with another half teaspoon of soda beaten into it; at the last add the well-beaten whites of two eggs. Put together with icing made from the remaining whites of eggs.

CHOCOLATE CAKE
Mrs. Kate Wilson

One cup of butter (scant) two cups sugar, yolks of seven eggs, or four whole ones, one cup of coffee, one teaspoon soda in coffee, one teaspoon baking powder in flour, and five tablespoons of chocolate. Cream butter and one cup of sugar; beat into this the eggs, beat well adding rest of sugar; stir in some of the coffee and some of the chocolate until all used. Lastly three cups of flour and flavoring. Bake in a large pan and frost. Tried and true.

CHOCOLATE MARSHMALLOW CAKE
Mrs. R. G. Emmel

One and one-half cups sugar, one-half cup butter, one cup water, two and one-half cups flour, two teaspoons baking powder, whites of five eggs; cream butter and sugar and add water and flour alternately in this proportion. One tablespoon water to two of flour.

FILLING

One-half pound marshmallows dissolved in one-fourth cup cold water in double boiler; add while hot beaten whites of two eggs, and-half cup chopped nuts of any kind spread between layers and on top, cover the whole with chocolate icing.

WHITE CAKE WITH CHOCOLATE FILLING
Mrs. T. Benton West

Two scant cups sugar, one cup milk, one cup butter, two cups pastry flour, one cup flour, two teaspoons baking powder, whites of six eggs, one teaspoon vanilia, for three layers. Filling: One cup sugar, one-fourth cup milk, one square grated chocolate; cook, beat and spread between layers.

CHOCOLATE CREAM
Susanna Marsh

Two cups of sugar, three cups of flour, two-thirds cup butter, scant, two teaspoons baking powder, one cup sweet milk, whites of five eggs. Cream butter and sugar, sift flour and baking powder three times, add a little of the milk and flour, alternately, until all is used, beating all the time; then fold in the whites of eggs beaten dry and ragged; flavor with vanilla. Put two-thirds of batter in two tins; into the other one-third grate six tablespoons of baker's chocolate and bake.

BLACK CAKE
Mrs. O. P. Johnston

Three eggs, two cups sugar, one cup molasses, one cup black coffee, one cup sour milk, two squares chocolate, one cup butter, one teaspoon each of cloves, cinnamon, two cups of raisins, two tablespoons vanilla, two teaspoons soda, four cups flour.

Maple icing for black cake: One pound maple sugar, one-half pint water; boil until it hardens in cold water, remove from stove and beat until it becomes light-brown in color; beat in one egg well beaten. Fine.

MAHOGANY CAKE
Mrs. S. G. Richards

One and one-half cups sugar, two cups flour, three eggs, one-half cup sweet milk, one-half cup butter, two teaspoons baking powder, one teaspoon soda, (level full) vanilla to taste; one-half cup grated baker's chocolate and one-half cup sweet milk thickened on the stove; when cool add to the above. Filling: One cup sweet milk, one cup sugar, butter the size of a walnut; cook until it shreds; beat and flavor with vanilla; spread over the top of the above loaf cake before it coats.

SPICE CAKE
Mrs. L. B. Myers

One and one-half cups sugar, one small cup butter, one cup milk, two cups flour, two heaping teaspoons baking powder, four eggs, yolks well beaten with sugar and butter. Beat whites to a froth and add last. One cup chopped raisins, one tablespoon molasses, one teaspoon cinnamon, one-half teaspoon cloves, one teaspoon vanilla, one-half cake grated chocolate. Bake in moderate oven. Filling: Two cups of brown sugar, one-half cup sweet milk, one-half cup butter; boil until it threads and beat until cool.

RIBBON CAKE
Alice Mathews

Cream together one cup butter and two of sugar, add four well-beaten eggs, one cup milk and three and one-half cups of sifted flour, to which has been added one heaping teaspoon baking powder; divide into three parts; to the first part add one tablespoon melted chocolate, and flavor with vanilla, the second with orange and to the third add a small quantity of fruit coloring, making as deep a pink as desired. Bake in layer cake tins; place orange layer at bottom and spread with boiled icing, then the brown spread likewise, lastly the pink. Have enough icing for the top to which a few drops of fruit coloring has been added.

HICKORY-NUT CAKE
Mrs. Chas. Jenks

One and one-half cups sugar, one-half cup butter, two-thirds cup sweet milk, two cups flour, two teaspoons baking powder, three eggs, one cup chopped meats. To be baked in two layers and put together with frosting.

SMALL LAYER
Mrs. C. C. Cunningham

One cup granulated sugar, one-half cup butter creamed with sugar, one-half cup sweet milk, one and one-half cups pastry flour, two teaspoons baking powder (very small), whites of four eggs beaten very stiff and added last. This makes two good layers.

CREAM CAKE
Emily S. Cooper

Two cups flour sifted with one level teaspoon soda four times, one cup sugar, two eggs, one cup sour cream, one teaspoon vanilla. Bake in three layers. Use any good filling or boiled icing.

West Side Public Square

CREAM CAKE
Mrs. C. C. Cunningham

On the beaten whites of ten eggs, sift one and-one half goblets of pulverized sugar and one goblet of flour through which has been stirred one heaping teaspoon of cream tartar. Stir very gently. Do not beat it. Flavor with one teaspoon vanilla. Bake in two large layers. For filling use whipped cream, sliced chocolate creams and English walnuts cut fine.

SATAN'S CAKE
Mrs. M. C. Bellamy

Grate one-third cake chocolate. Pour over it one-half cup of boiling water, add one teaspoon soda and let stand while stirring up the cake. For cake—two cups brown sugar, one-half cup butter, one small cup sour milk, two and one-half cups flour, two eggs, one teaspoon vanilla. Add chocolate mixture and bake in layers. For filling—take two cups brown sugar, one-third cup sweet milk, butter size of an egg.

CRACKER CAKE
Mrs. H. A. Shirer

One scant cup rolled nuts, one full cup rolled crackers, four eggs, one cup sugar, one teaspoon baking powder, one teaspoon vanilla. Ice with boiled icing.

KELLY ISLAND CAKE
Eva Belville

One cup butter, two cups sugar, three cups flour, four eggs, one-half cup milk, three teaspoons baking powder. Bake in jelly tins and put together with the following filling: Stir together a grated lemon, a large grated apple, an egg and a cup of sugar. Boil four minutes.

METROPOLITAN CAKE

Mrs. A. T. Looney

White part: One cup butter, one and a half cups soft white sugar, one-half cup sweet milk, two cups flour, whites of four eggs, one teaspoon cream of tartar, one-half teaspoon soda. Dark part: One-half cup butter, one-half cup molasses (sorghum), one cup sugar, one-half cup sweet milk, two cups flour, yolks of four eggs, one teaspoon cream of tartar, one-half teaspoon soda, one teaspoon each of nutmeg, cinnamon and cloves. Each part will make two layers. Fruit icing for above: One-half cup seeded raisins, one-half cup of dates, one half cup figs cut fine; grind all together; beat the white of one egg very stiff; add to the fruit, pour over all a syrup made of one cup granulated sugar and water to melt; cook until it thickens.

NEAPOLITAN CAKE

Ella McClure

White part:—One and a half cups sugar, half cup butter, half cup sweet milk, two teaspoons baking powder, whites of four eggs, two and a half cups flour. Dark part:—One cup brown sugar, half cup molasses, (or sugar only), half cup butter, two-thirds cup strong coffee liquid; one spoon baking powder, two and a half cups flour, one cup chopped raisins, one teaspoon cloves, mace and cinnamon. Bake. Put together in alternate dark and light layers. Filling:—One ounce grated chocolate, half cup sugar, two-thirds cup sweet milk; boil and let cool before spreading on; put one small teaspoon corn starch in the cream.

BLACKBERRY JAM CAKE
Mrs. Chas. Fagan, Ft. Madison, Iowa

One large coffee cup brown sugar, one-half cup butter, two and one-half cups flour, three eggs, three tablespoons clabber, one teaspoon soda, spices (all kinds), one cup blackberry jam. Bake in three layers.

MAPLE CAKE
Mrs. J. S. Bellamy

One cup butter, two cups sugar, three cups flour, whites of six eggs, yolk of one, three teaspoons baking powder and one of vanilla. Bake in three layers.

Filling: One and a half pounds maple sugar; Boil in one-half pint of water until it forms a ball when dropped in cold water. Remove from fire and beat a moment, then add two well beaten whites of eggs, beating all together until smooth and stiff. Spread over each layer and add a few chocolate creams and split almonds between layers and on top.

ORANGE CAKE
Mrs. Edith Ogle

One and one-half cups granulated sugar, one-half cup butter, one cup cold water, two heaping cups flour two teaspoons baking powder, whites of four eggs, yolks of three eggs, grated rind and juice of one orange. Use extra white of egg for plain icing.

CHOCOLATE COOKIES
Mrs. Edith Ogle

Two pounds sugar, one-half pound chocolate, three eggs, one cup sour milk, one-half teaspoon soda, twelve tablespoons butter or lard, two teaspoons each of cinnamon and cloves, one pound chopped almonds, flour enough to roll.

ALMOND LAYER CAKE
Mrs. C. C. Cunningham

One-half cup butter packed in solid, two cups sugar, cream with butter and add two and one-half cups pastry flour sifted with two even teaspoons baking powder and stir all together until like corn meal, then add one cup cold water and whites of four eggs beaten stiff. Bake in three layers. Spread boiled icing over each layer as you build the cake and sprinkle blanched almonds (split) over each layer.

Doughnuts   Em McCoy.

4 cups flour   2 cups l brown sugar
1 level teaspoon salt   3 heaping teaspoon B.P.
mix these ingredients dry then add one
cup of sweet milk and lastly 4 well beaten
eggs, flour to roll.

Spice Cake.   Villa's

1½ cups sugar   4 tablespoons mollasses
yelks of 4 eggs 1 cup shortening 1 cup sour
milk 1 teaspoon soda 2½ cups flour
spices and one cup raisins in filling.

Suet Pudding.   mrs. mac
1 cup each suet, mollasses and sour
milk, 1 teaspoon soda 3 cups flour and
1 cup raisins, 2 eggs steam 2½ hrs.

ICINGS

SIMPLE ICING
Irene Belville

To two cups pulverized sugar add enough cream to make into a smooth paste. Work until the lumps are all out and it is perfectly smooth and just thick enough to spread nicely. Add any desired flavor in quite a liberal quantity. If pink or any color is wanted add fruit coloring or add prepared cocoa to make brown icing.

ICING FOR CAKE
Mrs. T. G. Gilson

Beat the whites of four eggs, add four tablespoons of sugar. Boil one cup sugar wet with water, until it hairs, then beat into the eggs. Flavor.

ICING
Lila Marsh

A good, simple icing for little girls to make. You may use either the white of an egg or three or four tablespoons of either sweet cream or milk, and even water will answer, stirred to the proper consistency with sifted powdered sugar and flavored to suit.

FROSTING WITHOUT EGGS
Mrs. Gertrude McClymond

Five tablespoons milk, one cup sugar, stir until it boils, then boil five minutes without stirring, whip until nearly cold, spread quickly.

FILLINGS

OPERA CARAMEL FILLING
Mrs. W. P. Gibson

One and one-half cups brown sugar, one and one-half tablespoons butter, three-fourths cup thin cream. Cook until you can form a ball when tried in cold water. Beat until ready to spread.

MAPLE SUGAR FILLING
Mrs. E. W. Coxe, Red Oak, Iowa

One pound of maple sugar cooked with a little water until it threads, add whites of two eggs beaten. Beat until cool. Sprinkle chopped English walnuts between layers after spreading with maple sugar filling; then on top place half walnuts.

CHOCOLATE FILLING
Mrs. Dell McDonald, Des Moines, Iowa

One and one-fourth cups sugar, one and one-half blocks chocolate, butter size of an egg, one-half cup milk, one dessert spoon vanilla. Beat in water until hard.

MARSHMALLOW FILLING
Mrs. J. V. Brann

Boil two cups granulated sugar in one-half pint of water until it ropes, but not as hard as for other icings. Cut into small pieces one-half pound of marshmallows and stir into the sugar syrup and allow to boil well and beat until smooth. While hot pour into the above the whites of two well beaten eggs and mix thoroughly. Split one-half pound of Marshmallows and put between layers of cake and then pour over the icing or filling. Flavor to suit the taste.

LEMON FILLING
Mrs. Dell McDonald, Des Moines, Iowa

Two cups sugar, one egg, one large spoon of water. Piece and rind of one lemon. Stir all the time.

NUT FILLING
Mrs. Gertrude McClymond

One egg, one-half cup cream, one cup sugar, beat until light, then cook until thick, add one cup nuts, ground.

ALMOND FILLING
Mrs. J. V. Brann

One cup blanched almonds, one cup cream (sour or sweet), one cup white sugar, three eggs well beaten (or take yolks of four), one tablespoon corn starch or flour. Cook in double boiler and spread between layers. Beat until cool.

FEATHER CAKE
Carolyn Cooper

Two cups sugar, one-half cup butter and lard together, one cup sweet milk, beaten yolks of four eggs, three cups flour, sifted, two and one-half teaspoons baking powder, beaten whites of four eggs, flavor to taste. Bake in layers; use any icing desired.

COOKIES
Mrs. A. D. Steele

Two cups sugar, one cup butter and lard together, one cup cold water, two eggs, one teaspoon soda, season with nutmeg, flour to stiffen enough to roll.

FROZEN AND DAINTY DESSERTS

"I always thought cold victuals nice;
My choice would be vanilla ice."

LEMON ICE
Mrs. Hester Cunningham

Juice of two lemons, juice of one orange, one-half can grated pineapple, two cups sugar, one quart fresh milk, white of one egg. Freeze milk partly before adding other mixture.

LEMON ICE
Millie W. Baker, Chicago

Boil one and one-half pints sugar and two pints water till thick like syrup. Let cool, then add juice of two oranges, two lemons, one large banana washed through sieve, chop a few nuts and add. Dissolve one-half tablespoon of Knox's gelatine in little water, add, then freeze.

APRICOT ICE
Nora Neal

One quart of Monarch brand apricots, one lemon, one-half pound sugar, one quart of water. Boil sugar and water together for five minutes. Press apricots through a sieve, add them to the syrup, add juice of lemon and when cold freeze same as ice cream. When almost frozen add stiffly beaten whites of two eggs and two large spoons of rich cream.

Residence of J. W. Manhardt

ORANGE ICE
Mrs. G. K. Hart

Two oranges, one lemon, one quart fresh milk, one can of grated pineapple, sugar to taste, add the white of one egg when most frozen.

LEMON SHERBET
Vera Vawter

Four lemons, one quart milk or milk and cream mixed, one pint sugar. Put milk and sugar in freezer and chill; then add lemons.

CRANBERRY FRAPPE
Mrs. G. W. Baxter, Telford, Tenn.

Cook one quart of cranberries in one pint of water, strain and add one pint sugar. Cook until sugar is dissolved. When cold add the strained juice of two lemons. Freeze and serve with turkey.

WILD CHERRY AND ALMOND SHERBET
Mrs. L. S. Woodruff

One quart water and one pint white sugar, juice of one lemon, twelve sweet almonds blanched and pounded; a wine glass of wild cherry syrup. Freeze in freezer. When half frozen add the beaten whites of three eggs. Serve in glass cups.

ROMAN PUNCH
Mrs. Carl A. Reaver, Eldora, Iowa

Take one quart of water, two lemons, half cup of wine, one pound powdered sugar, four oranges and the whites of four eggs. Dissolve in a bowl the sugar, keeping out two tablespoons. Add the rind of one lemon and the juice of two, also the juice of the oranges. Mix well. Freeze in an ice cream freezer, and when half frozen add half cup wine and whites of four eggs well beaten, putting in the two tablespoons of sugar. The results when well frozen will be delicious.

APRICOT ICE CREAM
Mrs. C. C. Jones, Ft. Missoula, Mont.

One quart cream, three-fourths pound sugar, one quart apricots or one pint of canned. Boil half of the cream in boiler; when hot add the sugar and stir until dissolved. Take from the fire, add the remaining half of cream, and when cool freeze. Pare and mash the apricots and stir them quickly into the frozen cream. Turn the crank rapidly for five minutes, then remove the cover and pack.

CHOCOLATE ICE CREAM
Mrs. H. Shivvers

Scald one pint of new milk, add by degrees three-fourths pound of sugar, two eggs well beaten, five table-spoons of dissolved chocolate; beat well with an egg-beater, place over the fire and heat until it thickens well. Stir constantly. Set off and add one tablespoon of dissolved gelatine. When cool add one quart of rich cream, one-half of it well whipped, a little extract of vanilla and freeze.

MARASCHINO ICE CREAM
Mrs. G. W. Baxter, Telford, Tenn.

One quart milk, five eggs, one and a half cups sugar, one pint cream, flavoring, two dozen Maraschino cherries sliced, and add a little of the liquor. Heat milk, beat sugar and egg together until light. When milk has reached boiling point, pour over eggs and sugar, stir and return to double boiler and stir until it begins to thicken, but do not cook it; then strain into dish and set aside to cool. Turn into freezer when cool; when partly frozen add sliced cherries, one pint of cream (whipped if thick enough) then freeze.

STRAWBERRY ICE CREAM
Mrs. C. C. Jones, Ft. Missoula, Montana

One and one-half pints milk, and into this mix well beaten yolks of two eggs, sweeten to taste, boil and let cool, then add one quart of cream and one quart crushed strawberries. Sweeten and freeze.

LEMON SHERBET

Squeeze juice from three lemons and pour one pint of boiling water over the rinds. Let stand ten minutes. Mix two and a half cups sugar, the lemon juice and hot water and freeze just a little, or stir until cold. Then add one pint rich cream mixed with beaten whites of three eggs. Stir briskly until frozen. This quantity is sufficient for eighteen sherbet cupsful.

PINEAPPLE SHERBET
Marguerite Bellamy

Two pounds white sugar, two quarts water, six lemons, one large can sliced pineapple, strawberry juice and whites of four eggs. Cut the pineapple very fine, squeeze the juice from the lemons and soak in the water for two hours. Strain and add sugar and enough strawberry juice to color. Freeze until almost hard enough, then add the well-beaten whites of eggs, and finish freezing.

CARAMEL ICE CREAM
Cora Wolf

One quart new milk; whip three eggs to a foam; one cup sugar and three-fourths cup flour. Mix flour and sugar dry and take enough milk to dissolve them. Put this into new milk and cook, stirring all the time. While hot add one cup granulated sugar browned until it smokes, stir all the time. Put this into cooked part and add one-half gallon cream. Flavor with vanilla, one teaspoon full.

FROZEN PUDDING

Mrs. Sallie Cunningham

Three-fourths pint milk, one half cup sugar, one egg, one-fourth cup flour.   Put in a double boiler and cook same as custard; let get cold, then add one pint whipped cream.   Pour in moulds and pack well with ice.

ICE CREAM

Mrs. Jessie Bilby

Three quarts rather thin cream or use rich cream and milk, three small cups sugar, two tablespoons crystal flake gelatine, dissolved in a little cold milk.   Let sugar and a quart of the cream come to a boil; mix all together and flavor.   If well beaten when it begins to freeze this will make a gallon of smooth ice cream.

CHOCOLATE DRESSING FOR ICE CREAM

One-half cake of baker's chocolate, one pint of maple syrup, two cups of sugar, one cup of water.   Boil until thick as rich cream.   Serve ice cream in sherbet glasses, then put on top one tablespoon of the dressing (hot) and sprinkle with chopped almonds.

MAPLE MOUSSE

Mrs. L. S. Woodruff

Beat thoroughly the yolks of four eggs, add one cup of maple syrup and one cup of milk.   Place on stove and stir constantly until eggs thicken the syrup, then let it stand in a pan of ice water and beat until light and cool, add one and one-half pints whipped cream, give the whole a good beating and put into a well packed mould, using more salt than for packing ice cream. Chopped nuts may be added.   When done put into a freezer and freeze, then pack and let stand three or four hours.

CHERRY SHERBET

One quart canned cherries, juice of four lemons, one quart water, sugar to taste and freeze.

STRAWBERRY RELISH

Mrs. H. Shivvers

One quart strawberries, one pineapple cut in dice, chill and serve with whipped cream and powdered sugar.

RICE BLANC MANGE

Nora Elliott

One-half cup rice, cook in double boiler in one and one-half pints of milk and pinch of salt. Add one-half package of Jell-O, one-half cup powdered sugar. Set aside until it begins to thicken, then stir in one teaspoon vanilla, one-fourth cup sherry, one cup of stiff whipped cream. Turn into molds. Serve with whipped cream and candied cherries.

COMPOTE

One dozen sweet oranges, one cup sugar, juice of one-fourth lemon, one gill of water. Put sugar and water on to boil ten minutes, skim and add lemon juice. Peel oranges and cut in half crosswise; cut out core with a sharp knife. Put a few pieces at a time in the hot syrup and lay out singly on a hot dish, pour over them the remaining syrup, and stand on ice to cool. To dish pudding, lift can out of ice and carefully wipe salt off with towel dipped in boiling water. Put a round dish over top of it, turn upside down and remove can. Heap oranges on and around the pudding. Peaches may be used instead of oranges. This is a lovely dessert for a yellow and white luncheon.—From the Domestic Science Department at State University, Moscow, Idaho.

ANGEL PARFAIT
Myrtle Orcutt

Boil together without stirring one-half cup sugar and one-half cup water until it forms a soft ball in cold water, take off immediately and pour over the beaten whites of three eggs, beat until cold and spongy, add one teaspoon of vanilla, fold in one pint of whipped cream. Pack in freezer, but do not turn. Serve with candied cherries.

STRAWBERRY FLUFF
Luta Parsons

Strawberry fluff is very nice and is made of one and a fourth cups strawberries, one cup sugar, white of one egg. Put these ingredients in a bowl and beat with a wire whisk until stiff enough to hold its shape; this will require about thirty minutes. Pile lightly on dish, chill, surround with macaroons. Serve with cream sauce made of three-fourths cup heavy cream diluted with one-fourth cup milk, beaten until stiff, then add five and a half tablespoons powdered sugar, three-fourths teaspoon orange extract. If heavy cream is not used omit milk.

BANANA WHIP
Edna Bonebrake Williams, Guthrie Center, Iowa

Lay banana in the sweetened juice of one-half lemon. Pour over this whipped cream and serve with nuts or candied cherries.

PRUNE WHIP
Winnie Cotter

Cook until very tender, double handful of Oriole prunes, remove pits, chop fine, add one cup sugar, one cup chopped English walnuts, one teaspoon vanilla. Into this mix lightly the whites of eight eggs beaten stiff. Turn into loaf cake pan and bake in moderate oven about twenty minutes, or test with straw. Serve cold with whipped cream.

FLOATING ISLAND
Mrs. W. P. Gibson.

Place on stove one pint of milk. Beat whites of three eggs very stiff, drop into boiling milk by spoonsful. Let scald a moment and then turn. When scalded lift from milk, beat yolks with two tablespoons sugar, stir into boiling milk, remove from fire, flavor with orange or lemon. Pour carefully into dish with whites.

TAPIOCA
Mrs. S. F. Cole, Pella, Iowa

Soak one-half cup of tapioca until clear, put in a double boiler, add one cup of sugar, one-half teaspoon salt (level), two tablespoons dissolved cocoa and the last thing before taking from the fire stir in the beaten whites of two eggs; when ready to serve, serve with whipped cream.

SNOW PUDDING

Soak a package of Plymouth Rock Gelatine in one pint of cold water thirty minutes; add one and one-half pints hot water to dissolve, one and one-half cups sugar and two teaspoons lemon or other flavoring extract. Stir until sugar is dissolved; pour into a very shallow dish and set on ice until it slightly jells or thickens; beat to a stiff froth the whites of three eggs and a pinch of salt, beat in the gelatine until light and frothy and set back on ice until ready to serve. Sauce: Beat the yolks of the eggs with a cup of sugar and two teaspoons cornstarch. Scald one quart milk and turn it into the yolks, heat until it thickens, stirring all the time; add vanilla and a pinch of salt and let it cool. Using a little wine or brandy in the Snow pudding makes Princess Pudding.

FRUIT TAPIOCA
Mrs. G. E. McCorkle

Soak one cup of tapioca over night. In the morning cook in a double boiler in a quart of water until transparent. When done add cup of sugar, one tablespoon of lemon juice and three or four sliced bananas. Serve with plain or whipped cream. Other fruits may be substituted for bananas.

LEMON JELLY

Soak a package of Plymouth Rock Gelantine in one pint of cold water thirty minutes; then add two pints of hot water, one and one-half cups sugar (or sweeten to taste), two teaspoons lemon extract and stir until sugar is dissolved. Set on ice to harden and let it remain on ice until ready to serve.

ICED RICE PUDDING WITH COMPOTE OF ORANGES
Mrs. Millie M. Anderson, Lewiston, Idaho

Ingredients: One-half cup rice, one pint milk, one quart cream, one cup sugar,. yolks of six eggs, one teaspoon of vanilla. Two quarts of rock salt and ten pounds of ice are required for the freezing of same. Rub rice well in a clean towel, put on to boil in a double boiler in one pint of cold water; boil one half hour and drain, cover with milk and boil one-half hour longer. While this is boiling whip the cream. After whipping the cream all you can, add that which remains unwhipped to the rice and milk. Stand whipped cream in cool place until wanted. Press rice through wire sieve and return to double boiler in which it was cooked. Beat yolks and sugar together until light, then pour over the boiling rice, stir well, return to the fire and cook two minutes, or until it begins to thicken; take from fire, add vanilla and turn out to cool. When cool, put in freezer, and when frozen, add whipped cream, remove the dasher, smooth down and let stand packed two hours.

Residence of H. M. Dickerson

LEMON CREAM

Mrs. Gertrude McClymond

Into one and a half cups boiling water stir two tablespoons cornstarch, wet with water, and the juice of a large lemon, add the yolks of three eggs and one cup sugar; boil five minutes, then stir in the whites of eggs beaten stiff. Pour into sherbet glasses and serve cold with spoonful of whipped cream on top of each glass. Very nice without whipped cream.

PINEAPPLE TAPIOCA

Mrs. Bessie Boydston, Colfax, Iowa

Soak one large cup of tapioca over night, cook in double boiler until clear. Add two cups sugar and cook a few minutes. Remove from stove and add the juice of two lemons, one can of pineapple cut in very small pieces, and the beaten whites of two eggs. The juice of the pineapple may be added if it seems too thick. A few drops of red fruit coloring makes a pretty dish. Serve with whipped cream.

CUP CARAMEL CUSTARDS

Mrs. L. M. Cox, Pella, Iowa

Melt four tablespoons of sugar until a light brown, pour it into six custard cups and shake them quickly so that the caramel will line them. Beat three eggs without separating; add to them three tablespoons of sugar, and then a cup and a half of cream. Mix thoroughly, add a teaspoon of vanilla, and pour the mixture in the cups on top of the caramel. Stand them in a pan of hot water and bake in the oven ten or fifteen minutes, until they are set in the center. Turn out while hot on individual dishes and set aside to cool. Serve very cold.

STRAWBERRY CREAM
Mrs. J. J. Roberts

One quart strawberries rubbed through a fine sieve, mix with three pints of rich cream and sweeten. Whip to a froth, add one-half ounce dissolved gelatine, serve in sherbet glasses.

BIRD'S NEST PUDDING

Peel and core six or more apples, according to size, place in a shallow dish and fill the cores with sugar, bake until the apples are soft and tender. Make a plain jelly and when it begins to thicken pour it over the soft apple and place on ice until hard and ready to serve. Serve with grated nutmeg, sugar and cream. Nice with whipped cream. Particularly fine with pink gelatine.

JELLIES WITH NICE FRESH FRUIT

Pare and quarter or slice half a dozen or more ripe peaches, or other soft fruit, sprinkle with sugar and set one side. Soak a package of Plymouth Rock Gelatine in one pint of cold water thirty minutes; add one and one-half pints of hot water to dissolve it, then add one and one-half cups sugar, and lastly the fruit. Set on ice to harden and until ready to serve. Whole raspberries and strawberries are very nice this way.

ORANGE JELLY

Soak a package of Plymouth Rock Pink Gelatine in one pint of cold water thirty minutes; add two pints hot water, one and one-half cups sugar, flavor with orange extract, and stir until sugar is dissolved. Set on ice until wanted to serve. In a similar manner other jellies may be made, using extracts of raspberry, pineapple, strawberry, etc. In serving these jellies, cut across and across, breaking it up into crystals and piling it lightly in glass dishes. Eat plain or with cream and sugar; delicious with whipped cream.

VELVET CREAM
Mrs. Lafe S. Collins

One pint of cream whipped stiff, one-half package of gelatine soaked three hours in cold water, one-fourth can grated pineapple, one and one-half cups powdered sugar. Keep on ice.

COFFEE JELLY

Soak one package of Plymouth Rock Gelatine in one and one-half pints cold water thirty minutes; add one and one-half pints hot coffee and two cups sugar, and keep on ice to harden until ready to serve. Serve with sugar and cream.

MONARCH FRUIT JELLY
Winnie Cotter

One package of Bro-man-gelon, one pint cream before whipped, one pint boiling water, one small can Monarch pineapple, one small bottle Monarch cocktail cherries cut fine, one pound white grapes, cut in small pieces. Dissolve Bro-man-gelon in the boiling water; add fruit and when this begins to set add cream beaten stiff, set on ice until solid; cut in squares and serve with whipped cream.

PINEAPPLE FRUIT DESSERT
Anna Donley, Everist, Iowa

One pint whipped cream measured after whipping, one-half to one cup sugar, according to sweetness of pineapple, one coffee cup grated pineapple, one small bottle cherries, one cup almonds, blanched and halved, one-fourth box gelatine, boiled until dissolved in cup of water, one teaspoon vanilla. Beat lightly together, add beaten whites of two eggs; let get very cold. Serve with whipped cream and cherries on top.

MAPLE PUDDING
Mrs. G. W. Baxter, Telford, Tenn.

Soak one-half box of Knox's Gelatine in one cup of cold water, then set in hot water to dissolve. Add three-fourths cup of maple syrup and one pint of cream after it is whipped, nuts and pineapple. When it thickens put in cups to mold. When cold pour cooled Jell-O on top of each one. When solid place on plates and cover with whipped cream. Dainty and delicious.

APRICOT JELLY

Dissolve one package Orange Jell-O in one pint of boiling water. Just as it begins to stiffen, cover the bottom of any bowl with mixture; add a layer of apricots, previously stewed, sprinkle with English walnut meats broken in pieces. Then cover with more Jell-O. Make another layer as before of apricots and nut meats. Cover with Jell-O and set aside to harden. When firm remove from mold and serve with whipped cream.

ANGEL CHARLOTTE RUSSE
Mrs. Kate Crawford

One and one-half tablespoons Knox's Gelatine, one fourth cup cold water, one-fourth cup boiling water, one cup sugar, one pint cream (before whipped), one-half dozen rolled macaroons, one dozen marshmallows cut in small pieces, one small bottle cocktail cherries (cut small) three-fourths cup chopped nuts, flavor with vanilla. Soak gelatine in cold water and disolve in boiling water, add sugar. When this cools, add cream beaten stiff, nuts, macaroons, marshmarrows and cherries, flavor, turn into cold mold or flat pan, cut in squares, or serve in glasses with whipped cream; or remove the inside of an angel or sponge cake, fill with the mixture and serve cold.

BAVARIAN CREAM
Mrs. Gertrude McClymond

One quart sweet cream, yolks of four eggs, one-half ounce gelatine, one cup sugar, two teaspoons vanilla. Soak gelatine in just enough water to cover it for one hour; drain and stir into one pint of cream made boiling hot; beat yolks of eggs and sugar together and add to boiling mixture. Heat until it begins to thicken but not boil. Flavor. While hot stir in the other pint of cream (which has been whipped) a spoonful at a time until consistency of sponge cake. Put in mold in cold place.

MAPLE CHARLOTTE RUSSE
Mrs. Adah Gaiser

One pint whipped cream, three-fourths cup maple syrup, one-half box Knox's gelatine dissolved in one-half cup cold water. To this add the syrup and whipped cream. Then add any fruit (without juice), such as candied cherries, sliced pineapple cut in small pieces, white grapes cut in halves and seeds removed, also nuts. Set your pan in ice-cold water and beat all this until it commences to harden, then pour in any mold you wish and set on ice. Serve with whipped cream.

KRUMMED KUCHUS
Burnie Woodruff

One-half pound dates, one-half pound English walnuts (cut nuts in small pieces), one cup sugar, six eggs beaten separately, three tablespoons bread crumbs, one teaspoon baking powder. Mix baking powder with bread crumbs, add sugar, beat in the eggs, then fruit, spread in well buttered pans. Cut fruit in small pieces. Bake in dripping pans about twenty minutes. It is better to stand two or three days, but can be used soon as cold. Crumble it up and put on small plates, placing a tablespoon of whipped cream on each. This is delicious.

CHARLOTTE RUSSE
Luta Parsons

One quart sweet cream whipped to a froth, one-half box gelatine dissolved in milk, whites of five eggs beaten very stiff, one cup sugar. Flavor with vanilla.

MACAROONS
Laura Parsons

Beat the white of one egg to a stiff froth and add, gradually, six level tablespoons fine granulated sugar and five level tablespoons Pillsbury's Vitos, continue the beating. Flavor with teaspoon vanilla or lemon.

HICKORYNUT MACAROONS
Mrs. D. B. Cherry

Take whites of two eggs and stir in powdered sugar until almost too stiff to drop from spoon; add one cup rolled hickorynut meats and drop in small teaspoonful two inches apart on lightly buttered tin sheet; dip the finger tips in cold water and smooth the top and bake in rather cool oven; let stand until cool before removing from tins.

CHARLOTTE RUSSE
Mary Anthes

Dissolve one ounce of gelatine in one pint of milk by boiling, beat the yolks of four eggs, (sweetened) and stir them in while the milk is on the fire. When this is cooked to the consistency of custard strain into a bowl stirring constantly. Season one-half gallon of cream with wine, whip to a stiff froth and beat it in just as the custard (which should be seasoned with vanilla or rose-water) begins to congeal, pour into glass bowl lined with sponge cake.

DELICIOUS WHIPPED CREAM
Mrs. Velma Risser

One cup thick cream, white of one egg, three table-spoons sugar, one teaspoon vanilla. Whip altogether with egg beater on platter.

ROSETTES WITH CREAM AND NUTS

Take one pint whipped cream, add two tablespoons powdered sugar, five drops almond extract. Cover the rosettes thickly with the cream and cover top with chopped almonds. Serve with coffee or chocolate.

MARGUERITES
Mrs. Millie M. Anderson, Lewiston, Idaho

Boil one cup sugar and one-half cup water until the syrup will thread when dropped from the tip of a spoon. Remove to the back of the range and add five marsh-mallows cut into small pieces. Pour on the whites of two eggs beaten until stiff, then add two tablespoons shredded cocoanut, one cup English walnut meats broken into small pieces and one-fourth teaspoon vanilla. Spread saltines with this mixture and bake until deli-cately browned. These wafers should be eaten the day on which they are made.

MAMA'S KISSES
Mary Timmonds Hays

Whites of three eggs beaten stiff and dry, add five large cooking spoons of fine granulated sugar and one teaspoon vanilla. Stir lightly and just enough to mix thoroughly. Drop on paper placed upon an upturned dripping pan and bake in moderate oven twenty or thirty minutes. Speed is necessary in making these success-fully, as, if the kisses are not put into the oven as soon as the sugar and eggs are mixed, the former melts and the mixture will run over paper instead of keeping shape. Use small tablespoonsful in dropping.

PICKLES, CATSUPS AND REL-ISHES

"Who peppered the highest was sure to please."

MUSTARD PICKLES

This recipe was sent in by the following ladies: Mrs. D. A. McTag-gart, Mrs. P. M. Stentz, Mrs. J. W. Elliott, Mrs. J V. Brann, Mrs. J. D. Hanks, Miss Josie McKenzie, Mrs. S. J. Marsh.

Four quarts cauliflower broken apart well, four quarts onions cut small, or use small ones, four quarts cucumbers cut small, with one cup of salt and water to cover. Let stand over night. In the morning put on the stove and let come to a scald (but not boil), then drain out in a jar. Then take four quarts of Hawkeye vinegar (cider), four quarts sugar, one cup flour, butter the size of an egg, one quarter pound French mustard, four teaspoons celery seed, two teaspoons cinnamon, two teaspoons tumeric. Mix flour and tumeric with a little vinegar and bring all to a boil and pour over the pickles in the jar. They are then ready for use. This makes four gallons of pickles.

OIL PICKLES
Mrs. G. W. Baxter

Two-thirds cucumber sliced, one-third onion, celery seed, olive oil. Slice cucumbers and onions, sprinkle with salt, let stand three hours and wipe dry, perfectly dry, place in jars, sprinkle with celery seed, then pour cn cold vinegar and a 35c bottle of oil for one-half gallon of pickles. Put in nasturtium seed if liked.

Residence of Lafe S. Collins

CUCUMBER PICKLES
Mrs. Howard Cunningham

Fill quart jars with cucumbers, add one tablespoon salt and cover with good cold vinegar. Seal.

GREEN TOMATO PICKLES
Mrs. L. K. Butterfield.

Two gallons sliced green tomatoes, one dozen onions, two quarts brown sugar, two quarts vinegar, two tablespoons each black pepper, salt, cinnamon, cloves, whole mustard seed, celery seed and tumeric. Stew carefully until tender. Drain tomatoes over night before adding other ingredients.

OLIVE PICKLES OF CUCUMBERS
Mrs. J. H. Burma

One gallon cucumbers sliced fine, one teacup diamond crystal salt. Mix thoroughly, let stand over night. In the morning rinse, let drain. One ounce white mustard seed, one ounce black mustard seed, one tablespoon celery seed, one-half pint olive oil. Pour on vinegar enough to cover pickles, put in jars, alternating layer of cucumbers then layer of the mixed seeds. Pour oil over it and let stand a short time for oil to settle through. Pour on vinegar, cover with a plate. Stir well every two days for a week.

CUCUMBER PICKLES
Mrs. Marie Vawter

Gather and salt, pour boiling water over them, and let stand over night. Put vinegar on stove, sweeten to taste, let come to a boil. Have pickles wiped dry and placed in quart cans, with one teaspoon mixed spices for each quart, alum the size of a hazelnut, pour boiling vinegar over and seal immediately. Use good strong vinegar.

MUSK MELON PICKLES
Mrs. Bertha Black

Pare half ripe muskmelons (green ones will do.) Remove seeds, cut in slices, cover with vinegar and let stand 24 hours. For one gallon of fruit take one quart cider vinegar, one pound light brown sugar, one ounce cinnamon bark, whole cloves, one-half teaspoon mace. Add melons and let boil till tender. After boiling the syrup down pour over pickles. Celery seed added last gives these pickles a fine flavor.

CAULIFLOWER PICKLES
Mrs. W. V. Elliott

Boil three cauliflowers in salted water until tender. Place in jars, and pour over the following mixture: Two and one-half quarts vinegar, one and one-half cups sugar, one-fourth cup ground pepper, one-fourth pound ground mustard, one ounce butter, three eggs. Beat eggs, then add other ingredients. Boil all together. After taking from fire add one pint grated horseradish

CUCUMBER MANGOES
Mrs. G. W. Baxter, Telford, Tenn.

Pare ripe cucumbers and cut off small portion of ends. Fasten with tooth picks. Soak over night in one tablespoon of salt to quart of water. Drain and put in fresh water with alum size of walnut two hours. Remove ends and drain dry. One pound seeded raisins cut in two, one-fourth pound citron, one-half pound candied ginger cut fine, one half pound figs. Pack well in cucumber, sew on the ends and boil until clear in two pounds white sugar, one ounce stick cinnamon, one ounce whole cloves and piece of ginger root. Put in stone jar.

CHILI SAUCE
Mrs. T. G. Gilson

Take twelve large tomatoes, three green peppers, two onions, one tablespoon salt, two of sugar, one of cinnamon, three cups Hawkeye vinegar. Peel the tomatoes and onions, chop fine; cut the peppers in halves. Mix all together and boil two hours. Bottle and seal.

DELICIOUS PICKLES
Mrs. J. B. Elliott

Two quarts green tomatoes, one quart red tomatoes, three bunches celery, three large onions, three red sweet peppers, three green sweet peppers, one head cabbage, one large, ripe cucumber, half coffee cup salt. Chop all. Cover and let stand over night. Drain well and add three pints vinegar, two pounds dark brown sugar, one teaspoon mustard, one teaspoon pepper. Cook about one hour. Bottle or seal tight.

SWEET CUCUMBER MANGOES
Mary Anthes

Take medium sized cucumbers. Let them be in salt water nine days, then soak them in fresh water twenty-four hours. Open them lengthwise and take out seeds, place in preserving kettle with alternate layers of grape leaves, sprinkling a teaspoon of alum over each layer and cover with equal parts of vinegar and water; scald until green. Take lemons and cut in thin slices, including peeling, then fill the cucumbers with the slices of lemons and raisins, tie or sew together and place in jars, adding one-half ounce cloves and one ounce cinnamon bark broken in small pieces. Make a syrup of one pound sugar to one pint vinegar, boil and pour over cucumbers every morning for nine mornings, adding enough every time to thoroughly cover pickles.

CHOW CHOW
Mrs. E. Momyer

One gallon chopped tomatoes, one-half gallon chopped cabbage, one quart chopped onions. Put salt over each separate and let stand over night. Next morning drain off the brine. Put all together into a large kettle and cover with vinegar. Add two cups sugar and celery seed, cinnamon and other spices if desired. Cover tightly and simmer all well until it is cooked all through and seems tender. Put into bottles or glass jars.

BORDER SAUCE
Blanche Elliott

Two quarts green tomatoes sliced very fine (sprinkle with handful of Diamond Crystal salt, let stand over night), two quarts cabbage sliced very fine, one and one-half pints vinegar, one heaping cup sugar, five small onions sliced, two-thirds tablespoon tumeric, one-half tablespoon ground allspice, one-half tablespoon celery seed. Add vinegar, sugar, tomatoes and spices together and cook twenty minutes. Then add cabbage and onions and let boil up, remove from stove and pack in jars while hot.

CORN RELISH
Eva Belville

One dozen ears corn, one head cabbage chopped fine, one-half dozen green mango peppers, a few little red peppers cut in rings, one bunch of celery, one onion, mix together. Add following dressing after it has boiled ten minutes: Three pints vinegar, one-third pound mustard, one teacup sugar, some mustard and celery seed, salt to taste. After mixing the dressing with the other ingredients boil slowly about twenty minutes. Add more vinegar if necessary.

SALTED CHERRIES
Alice Mathews

After cherries have been thoroughly washed, place in quart jars leaving the stems on. Over the top spread one tablespoon salt. Cover with vinegar and seal.

TOMATO SAUCE
Flora Pitsor

Cook one can tomatoes, run through a sieve, add two tablespoons butter, one teaspoon sugar, salt and pepper to taste. Cook until thick. Splendid to serve on cold meats and especially on tongue.

COLD CATSUP
Ruby Gamble

One peck ripe tomatoes, three bunches celery, one cup sugar; one cup grated horseradish, one-third cup mustard seed, one-half cup salt, two red peppers, three pints vinegar, one spoon cloves, one cup chopped onions. Tomatoes, celery and peppers chopped fine.

CURRANT CATSUP
Burnie Woodruff

Five pounds currants crushed, three pounds light brown sugar, one pint good vinegar, two tablespoons ground cinnamon, one tablespoon each ground cloves and allspice, one-half teaspoon salt, one teaspoon black pepper. Boil just one hour, cool and bottle tight.

CHILE CON CARNE
Mrs. C. C. Cunningham

Six onions—two garlic onions—one pint tomatoes, one pound chopped meat, one pint beans, one tablespoon carminna seed, two tablespoons Chile powder, two tablespoons flour browned in one tablespoon of lard. Mix all and boil with a medium sized piece of suet.

MUSTARD FOR TABLE USE
Mrs. W. V. Elliott

One pint vinegar placed on stove. One and one-half tablespoons mustard, one tablespoon salt, one tablespoon sugar, five well-beaten eggs, walnut of butter. When thoroughly mixed, stir into warm vinegar and let come to a boil. Remove to cool and it is ready for use.

TOMATO CATSUP
Estella Wright

One-half bushel tomatoes and two large onions, boil three hours, strain out skins and seeds, add three pints vinegar, one teacup salt, one and one-half tablespoons cayenne pepper, four tablespoons allspice, five cups brown sugar. Put two tablespoons celery seed, three tablespoons whole cloves and two sticks cinnamon in separate muslin bags while it boils one hour or until thick enough to suit taste.

EGGS, CHEESE AND SAND-WICHES

"There is a best way of doing everything, even of boiling an egg."
—Emerson

OMELET
Mrs. J. M. Sloan

One cup milk, one cup bread crumbs, six eggs. Scald milk, pour over bread crumbs, fold over in pan and fry.

BAKED EGGS
Ella McClure

Into well-buttered gem pans break eggs, season with salt and pepper. Cover each egg entirely with grated cheese. Bake in moderate oven.

SCRAMBLED EGGS
Alice Bellamy

Four eggs broken in a dish, add two teaspoons cream for each egg, salt and pepper. Put a teaspoon butter in a frying pan. When very hot pour in eggs, etc., and at once stir with a fork until light and creamy.

EGG CROQUETTES
Mrs. G. W, Baxter, Telford, Tenn

One-half dozen hard boiled eggs, chopped quite fine; one tablespoon flour, one of butter rubbed together, then add one-half cup sweet milk and one cup bread crumbs. Cook altogether for a few minutes, let cool so you can handle, make in little cakes and dip in beaten egg and then in bread crumbs. Fry in hot lard or butter.

BAKED EGGS
Burnie Woodruff

Break into a large platter as many eggs as you need. Sprinkle with salt, pepper and lumps of butter. Set in the oven and in about five minutes the whites will be set and the eggs sufficiently cooked. A handy way on washing or ironing day when top of stove is in use.

CHEESE BREAKFAST RELISH
Nan Cornell

One cup milk, two eggs, one-half cup grated cheese, butter size of an egg, season with pepper and salt. Mix all together, place over fire, stir constantly; when thick serve at once with hot, crisp toast.

SUNFLOWERS
Iowa Sanitarium

Press the yolks and whites of hard-boiled eggs separately through a wire strainer. Pile the yolks in the center of a salad plate, placing the whites in a circle outside of it. Around this arrange shredded lettuce, piled lightly, and serve with a mayonnaise dressing. Two eggs for each three plates of salad will be sufficient.

EGG MOLDS
Selected

Six eggs, one-half teaspoon onion juice, one cup milk, one-half teaspoon chopped parsley, dash of pepper. Mix thoroughly, put in buttered molds. Bake or steam until center is firm. Serve with cheese sauce as follows: Two tablespoons butter, pinch of salt, one cup milk, two tablespoons flour, dash of pepper, one-fourth cup grated cheese. Blend butter and flour, add to hot milk. When cooked smooth add cheese, pepper and last salt.

Residence of Leopold Lüke

CHEESE STRAWS
Sue Reed

One cup cheese, one cup flour, one-half cup butter pinch of red pepper. Mix well, roll out, cut and bake in greased pans.

DREAMS
Lucy Bellamy

Slice bread in thin slices, place between in sandwich form slices of good fresh cheese, then fry in hot butter.

CHEESE WAFERS
Anna Findlay, Oklahoma City Oklahoma

Grate dry cheese, adding enough butter to make paste; spread on wafers rather thinly and brown in oven. These are delicious, warm or cold.

MACARONI AND CHEESE
Mrs John C. Myers

Break into small pieces one-half box macaroni, throw into six times the amount of boiling water and boil twenty minutes. Grate one pound of cheese. Put in baking dish one layer of macaroni, then cheese, salt, pepper and butter, then macaroni again, and so on until all are in the pan. Moisten with milk and bake one-half hour.

MACARONI AND CHEESE

Break about ten sticks of macaroni into inch lengths and boil in salted water twenty minutes. Take out in colander, pour cold water over it and let drain thoroughly. Make a sauce of one tablespoon butter, one tablespoon flour and one pint sweet milk. Spread a layer of grated cheese in the bottom of a baking dish, then a layer of macaroni and cover with the sauce; alternate the layers until dish is nearly full. Cover top with grated bread crumbs and bits of butter and set in oven until nicely browned.

PEANUT SANDWICHES
Mrs. W. C. Mentzer

Grind peanuts fine and moisten with mayonaise dressing. Spread thin slices of bread with butter, then with peanut filling.

NUT SANDWICHES
Mrs. W. P. Gibson

Mix equal parts grated cheese and English walnuts. Season with salt and cayenne. Spread between thin slices of buttered bread cut in fancy shapes.

NUT SANDWICHES
Anna Findlay, Oklahoma City, Oklahoma

Grate any kind of nut meats, mix with a little cream, add a pinch of salt, spread on thin slices of buttered brown bread.

NUT AND RAISIN SANDWICHES
Mrs. W. P. Gibson

Use equal quantity English walnuts and layer raisins. Stone raisins and chop together with nuts. Use between thin slices of graham bread and butter.

RIBBON SANDWICHES
Mrs Fred Reed, Elkhart, Indiana

Take thin slices of bread, butter them on both sides, place layers of deviled ham between, then press the entire sandwich, cut crosswise, making them ribbon-like sandwiches.

PEANUT BUTTER FOR SANDWICHES
M. M. G.

Shell and skin freshly roasted peanuts and grind to a powder, add to one half cup butter and work to a smooth paste. This is a very large quantity. It can be packed in a jar and kept for days. Nice for sandwiches.

HAM SANDWICHES
Mrs. Ella Everett

Ten cents worth cold boiled ham, five cents worth salted peanuts, four or five sweet pickles, grind each and mix with mayonnaise dressing. Spread between thin slices of buttered bread.

WELSH RAREBIT
Lucy Bellamy

Cut in pieces one half pound of soft cream cheese, melt slowly with one-half tablespoon butter, add one-half cup milk and two eggs beaten enough to mix well, but not light. Cook until it thickens, stirring constantly to prevent stringing. Season with salt and pepper, and serve at once on toast or hot waffles.

FRENCH SANDWICHES
Mrs. W. P. Gibson

One cup butter, two cups sugar, two cups flour, five eggs. Mix like sponge cake. Spread a thin layer of the batter on a deep cake tin with straight sides and over this put a layer about one inch deep of figs, currants and raisins, chopped. Pour rest of batter over this and bake in moderate oven. Let the cake cool in the tin.

CHEESE BALLS
Mrs. P. H. Donley, Wichita, Kansas

Mix one and one-half cups grated cheese with one tablespoon flour, season with one-third teaspoon salt, one-eighth teaspoon mustard, and cayenne pepper to taste. Fold into this the whites of three eggs beaten stiff and dry. Shape into balls size of hickory nuts. Roll in cracker meal or fine bread crumbs and fry in deep fat. Drain on brown paper and serve with salad course.

BEVERAGES

A CUP OF TEA

Put a teaspoon of Tone Bros. Cosmos tea in the pot and cover with one cup of boiling water; serve in a few minutes.

COFFEE

May Craddick-Hare, Milwaukee, Wisconsin

To make coffee for twenty-five, use thirty heaping tablespoons of Tone Bros. coffee, mixed thoroughly with the white of egg. If it seems too dry to mix easily, add two or three tablespoons of cold water and let it stand a few minutes, then add eight or ten cups of hot water, and let it all come to a boil as slowly as possible, then add the rest of the boiling water, put on back of stove where it will not boil, dash a very little cold water in, let stand three to five minutes, and serve at once. Never let coffee boil hard. Use good coffee; cover well while making, that no strength can escape.

WATER CHOCOLATE

Mrs. J. A. J. Powers, Everist, Iowa

Two squares of Baker's chocolate, one quart of water, boil hard for three minutes and then add one rounded tablespoon of corn starch wet with cold water, three-fourths of a cup of sugar, and one teaspoon of vanilla; let all boil together for a few minutes, and serve hot with whipped cream which has been slightly sweetened.

FRAPPE
Alice Bellamy

Three dozen lemons, two dozen oranges, two large cans pineapples, strawberry juice, water enough to make five gallons and sugar to taste.

FIG PRUNE CEREAL

For each cup use one heaping teaspoon of Fig Prune cereal and the necessary boiling water. Boil ten minutes, using care to see that pot does not boil over. Slow and steady boiling much improves the flavor.

CHOCOLATE
Edna Bonebrake-Williams, Guthrie Center, Iowa

Shave two squares of Baker's chocolate in pan, add three tablespoons sugar, pinch of corn starch and little water. Thoroughly dissolve, then add five cups of milk. Let it come to a boiling point. Serve with or without whipped cream.

EGG LEMONADE
Oskaloosa King's Daughters Cook Book

In one pint of water dissolve half pound of granulated sugar, squeeze in the juice of four lemons and add half a cup of cracked ice. Beat yolks and whites of four eggs separately until stiff. First add yolks, then whites. If necessary add more sugar. Nourishing and refreshing.

CHOCOLATE
Rebekah Imogene Bellamy

One tablespoon of grated chocolate to each person, one-half tablespoon of sugar, one cup of rich milk. Mix sugar and chocolate and add enough boiling water to dissolve. Let milk come to a boiling point and stir in the chocolate. Beat until it boils and serve with a tablespoon of whipped cream in each cup.

GRAPE WINE

Mrs. Fred. Grant

Fill a five-gallon jar two-thirds full of nice grapes. Remove about one-half of the stems, mash them, pour over one quart water. Let stand one week. Pour off juice and put in fifty cents worth of sugar (white). Fill bottles, leave uncorked until fermentation ceases. Keeps for years.

BLACKBERRY CORDIAL

Mary Anthes

One quart blackberry juice, one pound white sugar, three and one-half ounces grated nutmeg, one-half ounce powdered cinnamon, one-fourth ounce allspice, one-fourth ounce cloves, one pint best brandy. The spices in thin, muslin bags. Boil juice, sugar and spices together fifteen minutes, skimming well; add the brandy. Set aside in a closely covered vessel to cool. When perfectly cold strain and bottle, sealing the corks.

GRAPE JUICE

Gertrude McClymond

Carefully stem ripe grapes. Wash them. Drop into preserving kettle and barely cover with cold water. Cover, bring gradually to a boiling point and boil twenty minutes; take from the fire, mash and stir and then strain through a cheese-cloth bag to remove seeds and skins. Cleanse kettle, measure and return the juice of the grapes. Add to juice one-half cup of sugar to each quart of juice. Return kettle to stove and boil for five minutes. Strain a second time and while hot turn into bottles; cork and seal while hot.

RASPBERRY VINEGAR
Knoxville Congregational Cook Book

Put enough vinegar over mashed berries to cover them; let remain in cellar three days. Strain juice, and to one quart of juice add one pint of sugar. Let boil a few minutes, then seal in bottles air tight. When used, pour three or four tablespoons in glass containing crushed ice, then fill with water.

SWEETMEATS AND DAINTIES

"My mission in life is a sweet, I claim
For the children's eyes brighten at hearing my name."

FUDGES
Mrs. G. W. Baxter, Telford, Tenn.

Two cups sugar (one white, one brown), one cup milk, butter size of an egg.

FUDGES
Mrs. G. K. Hart

Two cups sugar, one of milk, lump of butter size of walnut, one-fourth cake of chocolate, pinch of soda; when done beat thoroughly after taken off the stove.

MOLASSES TAFFY
Isabel C. Hays

One quart molasses, one cup sugar, butter half the size of an egg. Boil over slow fire until it will harden when dropped in cold water, stirring often to prevent burning. Just before taking from fire, put in a half teaspoon soda and stir well; then pour it out into well buttered pans. When partly cooled pull.

A NICE CANDY
I. H. Garretson

Take one pound good "C" sugar; put in a vessel one teacup water, then add sugar; set over a slow fire until sugar is melted, when fire may be increased; when nearly done the syrup will throw up flat bubbles. Let boil until a drop of the mixture is brittle and will break in the fingers when dropped into cold water. Remove from fire at once and pour thin into greased plates. Let cool, then pull white.

High School Building

BUTTER SCOTCH

Mrs. George Underhill.

Two cups brown sugar, one-half cup water, boil until dropped hard in cold water, then add butter size of a goose egg, flavor with vanilla. Do not stir. Pour into greased pans to cool.

CREAM CARAMELS

Mrs. Margaret Roberts.

Put one-fourth pound of chocolate, one-half pint of cream, one pint of granulated sugar into a saucepan and stir until it boils, then stir constantly until the mixture forms a soft ball when dropped into cold water. Begin to test after the first ten minutes. Pour into greased pans, and when cold cut into inch squares.

VANILLA CARAMELS

Gail Gilson

Two cups granulated sugar, two-thirds cup sweet milk, filled with butter not melted, stir until it begins to boil; not again. Cook over slow fire about twenty-five minutes or until it turns a light brown. Flavor. Pour out on buttered tins and when pretty nearly cooled mark off in squares.

FINE CANDY

Mrs. Anthes.

Three cups granulated sugar, one-half pint of Golden Drip syrup, three-fourths pint cream, ten cents worth of candied cherries, one cup English walnuts. Beat cream, sugar and syrup together, then boil, stirring all the time. When done add cherries, chopped nuts and vanilla. Beat the same as fudges.

CREAM CANDY
Mrs. T. S McClymond.

One cup granulated sugar, one-half cup milk.   Boil until it begins to thicken, then beat.   Thicken with powdered sugar, roll, add two or three drops pink coloring, Flavor to taste.   Make three times.   Color one with chocolate, leave one white.   Roll one layer, put other color on top of first and roll, place third on top of second and roll, cut in squares.

SEA FOAM
Gail Gilson

Boil one cup granulated sugar and one cup dark brown sugar in one-half cup of water until it hairs;   beat into the white of one egg well beaten, and flavor.   Beat it until firm and drop on buttered pan with spoon. Chopped English walnuts improve it.

FRENCH NOUGAT
Mrs. R. S. Granger, Eureka Springs, Arkansas

One cup granulated sugar and a little water, boil as for icing, beat into the beaten whites of three eggs, keep beating slowly all the time.   In another vessel have three cups granulated sugar, one cup of glucose and one cup of water, boil and when hard in water, beat into the other.   Three cups of nuts.   Flavor.

CANDY WAFERS
Mrs. Marie Vawter

Two large cups granulated sugar, one-half cup water, one large tablespoon glucose.   Mix well and let boil six minutes.   Remove from stove, divide into parts, flavor one with wintergreen mixed with four or five drops red fruit coloring.   The other flavor with peppermint.   Beat until cool enough to drop on a marble or oil cloth with a teaspoon.

DIVINITY

Mrs. Fred Grant

Six cups granulated sugar, one pint of Silver Drips, two pounds English walnuts, one and one-half pints of cream and milk, one-half teaspoon cream tarter.

SIMPLE CANDY

Helen Cooper

One cup dark brown sugar, one cup granulated sugar, one-half cup cream or milk, one tablespoon butter. Boil without stirring five minutes, or until it will form a soft ball when tested in cold water. When done take from fire, add one teaspoon vanilla, stir until cool and pour into plates.

PENOCHE

Mrs. M. D. Woodruff

Two cups light brown sugar, one cup sweet cream cooked together until it will roll into a ball when put into water. When nearly done burn two tablespoons of white sugar and stir in. Add nuts after removing from fire. Beat thoroughly and pour into buttered pans. Cut into squares.

MARSHMALLOWS

Gail Gilson

Dissolve 2 tablespoons of Knox's gelatine in six tablespoons of water. Boil two cups of granulated sugar in six tablespoons of water until it hairs; beat into gelatine and add the white of one egg well beaten. Beat. Butter the pan, sprinkle with pulvurized sugar, pour in marshmallows and cover the top with sugar. When cool cut in squares.

STRAWBERRY FLOAT
May Collins McCorkle

One pint strawberries and one pint sugar mashed together. Beat stiff the whites of three eggs and add gradually the berries. Continue to beat until the mixture will stand alone. Place in glass dish and keep in cool place until served.

GRILLED ALMONDS
Mrs. Dixie C. Gebhardt

Blanch a cupful of almonds, dry them thoroughly Boil a cup of sugar and a quarter of a cup of water till it hairs, then throw in almonds; let them fry, as it were, in this syrup, stirring them occasionally. They will turn a faint yellow brown before the sugar changes color. Do not wait an instant once this change of color begins, or they will lose flavor. Remove them from fire and stir them until the syrup has turned back to sugar and clings irregularly to the nuts. You will find this a delicious change from the salted almonds.

FRUITS

"The best of households have their 'Family Jars.'"

CANNING FRUIT

Contributed by request

Time for boiling	Sugar to quart.
Cherries five minutes	Six ounces
Raspberries six minutes	Four ounces
Blackberries six minutes	Six ounces
Strawberries eight minutes	Eight ounces
Plums ten minutes	Eight ounces
Rhubarb, sliced ten minutes	Ten ounces
Quinces fifteen minutes	Ten ounces
Pears, halved twenty minutes	Six ounces
Peaches, halved eight minutes	Four ounces
Peaches, whole fifteen minutes	Four ounces
Siberian crab apples twenty-five minutes	Eight ounces
Sour apples, quartered ten minutes	Five ounces

TO CAN RED RASPBERRIES

Nan Cornell

Fill jar, shaking them down until can is as full as possible. Have boiling syrup; pour over until fruit is covered; seal. Stand cans in iron kettle, completely covering cans with boiling water, cover up tightly until cold.

HEAVENLY JAM
Mrs. C. W. Cornell

Five pounds currants, five pounds sugar, one pound chopped raisins, two lemons cut in small pieces, boil one hour; seal in jars. Delicious.

CHERRY PRESERVES, RASPBERRY OR STRAWBERRY JAM
Mrs. Jessie Bilby

Drain berries. Of any of the above fruits take two quarts and two quarts sugar. Do not cook more than this amount at one time. For berries do not measure sugar so liberally as fruit. Put over hot fire. Stir gently and cook for twenty or twenty-five minutes.

RIPE GRAPE JELLY

Stem, wash, put in a stone jar, stand the jar in a kettle of boiling water, and boil until the grapes are soft. Strain through a jelly bag, allow granulated sugar pound for pound (or a pint for a pint), boil twenty or thirty minutes, add the sugar which should have been heated and boil five minutes longer. Pour in glasses. Seal when cold.

GREEN GOOSEBERRY JELLY
Mrs. W. R. Myers

Put the berries, after washing and stemming, in a pan and cover with water; place a plate upon them to keep them down, and cook till soft; then strain them through muslin or a very fine sieve, leaving them to drain a while. To each pint of juice allow three-fourths of a pound sugar and boil together, skimming occasionally till the jelly appears firm if a little be put on a plate. Pour into glasses. The berries are better when a few have begun to ripen.

CONSEVIRS
M. M. G.

One quart rhubarb without peeling, one pint red raspberries, one pint red currants, one pint chopped English walnuts, two oranges, one pound raisins, two lemons with peel. To each pound of fruit add a pound of sugar. Cook until thick like jelly.

PEACH PRESERVES
Mrs. H. N. Keables, Pella, Iowa

Pare and cut peaches into small pieces, cover one heaping pint bowl of peaches with one level pint of sugar let stand a few minutes, then bring slowly to a boil, and boil rapidly until transparent, then add one-half cup of blanched and shaved almonds, just heat the nuts through and seal.

TO CAN STRAWBERRIES
Dickie Cornell Gebhardt

Stem berries, picking out bruised or imperfect ones for jam. Wash carefully. To two boxes or quart bowls of berries use two cups granulated sugar and enough water (sparingly used) to start them cooking. Do not stir and bruise berries. Cook eight minutes. Can in quart jars, wrap well in paper and keep in dark, dry place until ready for use.

SPICED PEACHES
Mrs. A. T. Looney

To eight pounds fruit allow four pounds sugar, three pints of vinegar, two ounces stick cinnamon, one ounce cloves. Boil sugar, vinegar and spices five minutes, then add a few peaches at a time. When they can be easily pierced with a straw, place in a jar and add others to the vinegar until all have been cooked. Boil the syrup down a little more and pour over the fruit. Seal at once.

APPLE JELLY
Mrs. Adda Roberts

Quarter, but do not peel or core tart, juicy apples, almost cover with water. Stew till tender, let drain all night an a jelly bag. Boil the juice and for every pint of liquid add three-fourths pound sugar that has been heated. Boil until it congeals when dropped on a plate. A rose-geranium leaf dropped in each glass before pouring in the hot jelly gives a delicious flavor, but should be left in but a few minutes.

First Presbyterian Church

COOKERY FOR SICK.

"Simple diet is the best; for many dishes bring many diseases."—Pliny.

OATMEAL GRUEL
Mrs. Sarah Hamilton

Put four tablespoons of oatmeal into a pint of boiling water. Let it boil gently and stir often until it becomes as thick as you wish it. Then strain it and add to it while warm, butter, or sugar or wine, or whatever is thought proper to flavor it. Salt to taste.

FRUIT SOUP
Iowa Sanitarium

Cook one-half cup of sago in a double boiler until it is clear. Remove from fire and thin with one pint of cherry juice and a pint of blackberry juice. Add the juice of one lemon and one orange cut in dice, one cup of cherries and one cup of plums. Both the fruit and the juice may be varied according to taste.

CORNMEAL GRUEL
Mrs. Dickie Cornell Gebhardt

Two tablespoons of sifted cornmeal. Wash in cold water, draining off water each time, till after repeated washings, water drained off is clear. Add pinch of salt, pour over meal one pint boiling water and turn into saucepan to boil gently for half an hour. Thin with boiling water and stir frequently. When done add a tablespoon of cream (after straining), but if patient's stomach is weak it is best without. Some like it unstrained and sweetened.

CREAM CHICKEN SOUP
Dickie Cornell Gebhardt

Mix yolks of two eggs with two tablespoons of cream; add slowly while stirring constantly, a small cup of hot chicken broth. Season to taste with salt. Pour the cream broth into a hot cup and serve with toast or crackers.

BOUILLION SUPREME
Mrs. H. L. Bousquet.

One of the best of light soups: Cook two tablespoons of tapioca in two quarts of bouillion until it is smooth but not thick. When it is done (in about half an hour) put the yolks of raw eggs (one to every two persons) in the bottom of the tureen; pour on the hot soup and beat to a frothy cream.

STEAMED EGG
Iowa Sanitarium.

Separate the egg, beat the white to stiff froth, then add to it the slightly beaten yolk. Turn into a suitable dish for serving, and place in a pan containing boiling water. Remove this from the stove, cover closely to retain the steam, and leave for five or ten minutes until the egg is lightly cooked. Serve hot.

STEWED CRACKERS
Tested

Split two or three cream crackers and put them in double boiler or a bowl set in a pan of hot water. Pour over them boiling water to cover and add a pinch of salt; cook until they look clear or nearly transparent, being careful that there should be enough water to cover them during the cooking. Slip them into a hot serving dish without breaking and serve with sugar and cream.

SOMETHING FOR A NIGHT LUNCH
Recommended by N. R. C.

Beat up a fresh egg with a grain of salt, pour upon it a pint of boiling milk, stirring all the time; serve hot. Taken alone or with dry toast this is excellent nourishment for an invalid needing food during night.

SCRAPED BEEFSTEAK
Mrs. Sarah Hamilton

Lay a tender steak on meat board, then with a silver knife scrape all you can from one side. Turn steak and do likewise on the other side; after you have scraped all, make into little cakes, roll in flour or cracker crumbs and fry in hot butter.

EGG LEMOMADE
Jennie Johnson, Des Moines, Iowa

Beat the yolk of one egg lightly. To this add the juice of one-half lemon and two ounces of water, straining through a small sieve; sweeten to taste and turn into a glass. Beat the white of one egg to a stiff froth, add one teaspoon sugar and add to the lemonade. Stir together and serve.

STUFFED POTATO
Jennie Johnson, Des Moines, Iowa

Prepare and bake a large smooth potato. Cut evenly three-fourths of an inch from the end, and scrape out the inside, taking care not to break the skin. Season with salt and a little thick cream, or cocoanut cream, being very careful not to have it too moist, and beat thoroughly with a fork until light; fill the skins with potato, fit the broken portions together and reheat in oven. When heated throughout, wrap the potatoes in squares of white tissue paper fringed at both ends. Twist the ends of the paper lightly together above the fringe and stand on end with the cut end uppermost.

AN EGG ON TOAST
Mrs. Sarah Hamilton

On a delicately toasted slice of bread place the well beaten white of an egg. Drop into this beaten white the unbroken yolk. Sprinkle with a little salt, and set in a hot oven. Then remove when white browns nicely. Add little bits of butter if desired.

APPLE CUSTARD
By request

For one person: Pare, quarter and stew until tender one apple in a thin syrup of water and sugar. Remove and place in a sauce dish. To the syrup add juice of half an orange and beaten yolk of one egg. Boil until this thickens, remove and stir in beaten white of egg; pour over apple and serve cold.

A CUP OF CUSTARD
Mrs. Sarah Hamilton

Into a large coffeecup pour one well-beaten egg. Fill cup with sweet milk, sweetening to taste. Flavor with a bit of grated nutmeg. Place cup in a deep pan of boiling water; place in oven. Watch closely and remove from oven as soon as it sets.

TO PREPARE RICE FOR AN INVALID
Mercy Hospital, Des Moines, Iowa

Have one pint of boiling salted water in a double boiler; put half teacup of rice into a clean baking pan and parch in a moderate oven until rice begins to turn a light yellow; stir it while very hot into the boiling water and boil rapidly for twenty or thirty minutes. Cooked in this way rice is never sticky, is partly predigested and tastes better.

HOUSEHOLD HINTS

Ripe tomatoes will remove stains from the hands.

Tea stains and many fruit stains may be removed by pouring boiling water through the stain.

To extract ink from cotton, silk or woolen goods, dip the spots in spirits of turpentine and let it remain for several hours, then rub thoroughly between the hands.

Machine grease may be removed from wash goods by dipping the spot in cold rain water and soda.

A paste made of raw starch and cold water will remove blood stains. Let this remain on several hours.

Spots of rust or mildew may be removed by wetting with lemon juice and holding it over steam of teakettle.

A little butter rubbed on the tip edge of cream pitchers prevents the cream from dropping.

Make starch with soapy water, which gives a better gloss to the linen.

Keep a chamois skin for mirrors alone. Dip the skin in water containing a little alcochol, and wipe mirror.

Coarse salt and vinegar will clean enamel ware that has been burned or discolored.

Before using a new broom dip it in boiling water and let stand until water cools.

Flour the cake pan after greasing it if you do not want the cake to stick or burn.

For a nice looking pie sprinkle sugar and a little water over before baking

TO PRESERVE EGGS

Take one pint lime, one pint coarse salt. Pour over this three gallons boiling water. Let stand twenty-four hours. Place eggs in a stone jar and cover with the clear fluid.

TO WASH LACE CURTAINS

Let your curtains soak in cold water all day. In the evening put in one-half boiler hot water, one cake good soap, one teaspoon borax, one tablespoon turpentine, two tablespoons ammonia. Let soak over night and put through two or three clear waters. Starch and put on stretchers. Do not rub.

GOOD HAND LOTION

Two ounces glycerine, one ounce alcohol, one-fourth ounce gum tragacanth, one-half ounce rosewater, one pint soft water. Let gum tragacanth soak two days in soft water, add glycerine and rosewater, strain and add alcohol.

COSMETIC JELLY FOR THE HANDS

Soak sixty grains of whole gum tragacanth in fourteen ounces of rosewater for two days; strain forcibly through muslin, and add one ounce each of alcohol and glycerine. Perfume to suit. Use immediately after bathing.

GOOD COUGH REMEDY

Four ounces wild cherry bark, one pint apple brandy, four ounces mullein leaves, one and one-half pounds rock candy. Put wild cherry bark in brandy and let stand five to seven days. Put mullein leaves in half gallon water, simmer all day on slow fire, then strain. Add candy to mullein water and boil to half quantity, then add brandy and boil slightly.

CREME MARQUISE

One quarter ounce white wax, two and one-half ounces spermaceti, two and one-half ounces oil of sweet almonds. Melt, remove from fire, add one and one-half ounces rosewater. Beat till creamy, not till cold. Be sure that your druggist give you only one-fourth ounce white wax. More will make it too hard.

ASTRINGENT WASH
(For Coarse Pores, Oily or Flabby Skin.)

Take a half pint bottle and in it put one and one-half ounces cucumber juice, half fill the bottle with elder flower water, add one ounce of eau de colonge and shake well. Then add one-half ounce simple tincture of benzoin. Shake slightly and fill with elder flower water. Apply with soft sponge night and morning.

ORANGE FLOWER SKIN FOOD
(For Wrinkles.)

One-half ounce white wax, one-half ounce spermaceti, one ounce cocoanut oil, one ounce lanoline, two ounces oil of sweet almonds. Melt in a porcelain kettle; remove from heat and add one ounce of orange flower water, three drops tincture of benzoin. Beat briskly with egg-beater until creamy.

INDEX